MIDDLEBURY COMMUNITY SCHOOLS
EXPLORE

Jacob's Ladder
READING
COMPREHENSION
PROGRAM

GRADE
5

Nonfiction

Jacob's Ladder
READING COMPREHENSION PROGRAM

Nonfiction

GRADE

5

Joyce VanTassel-Baska, Ed.D., &
Tamra Stambaugh, Ph.D.

PRUFROCK PRESS INC.
WACO, TEXAS

Prufrock Press Inc.
P.O. Box 8813
Waco, TX 76714-8813
Phone: (800) 998-2208
Fax: (800) 240-0333
http://www.prufrock.com

Table of Contents

Acknowledgments

We would like to thank Lacy Compton and Stephanie McCauley from Prufrock Press for their unwavering support of this project and their dedication to helping us find appropriate nonfiction selections for this series. If age-appropriate passages were not available, they often rewrote items or found alternatives on similar topics. Their patience, responsiveness, and hard work are most appreciated.

Part I: Teachers' Guide to Jacob's Ladder Reading Comprehension Program

Rationale

Decoding and constructing meaning of the written word are two of the earliest tasks required of students in schools. These skills occupy the central place in the curriculum at the elementary level. Yet approaches to teaching reading comprehension often are "skill and drill," using worksheets on low-level reading material. As a result, students frequently are unable to transfer these skills from exercise pages and apply them to new, higher level reading material.

The time expended to ensure that students become autonomous and advanced readers would suggest the need for a methodology that deliberately moves students from simple to complex reading skills with texts matched to reading level as determined by Lexile and other approaches to ensure appropriate reading challenges. Such a learning approach to reading skill development ensures that students can traverse easily from basic comprehension skills to higher level critical reading skills, while using the same reading stimulus to navigate this transition. Reading comprehension and knowledge acquisition are enhanced by instructional scaffolding, using strategies and processes to help students analyze passages (Villaume & Brabham, 2002). In addition, teachers who emphasize higher order thinking through questions and tasks (like those applied in this program) promote greater reading growth (Taylor, Pearson, Peterson, & Rodriguez, 2003), especially when this instruction is presented through inquiry and discussion as opposed to isolated worksheet-like activities. Cognitive science suggests that students need to have purpose and direction for discussions of text to yield meaningful learning and that scaffolding is a necessary part of enhancing critical reading behavior and developing expertise (Bransford, Brown, & Cocking, 2000).

The Jacob's Ladder Reading Comprehension Program: Nonfiction series was written in response to teacher findings that students have a deep curiosity to learn more about the world around them, but need more developmentally appropriate materials and scaffolding to process and accurately interpret informational texts (Duke, Bennett-Armistead, & Roberts, 2003; VanTassel-Baska & Stambaugh, 2006a). Tivnan and Hemphill (2005) studied reading reform curricula in Title I schools and found that few of the reading programs emphasized skills beyond basic phonemic awareness, fluency, or limited comprehension. To compound this, many popularized reading curricula include less than 20% informational reading selections (Duke et al., 2003). For students who are in the lowest SES schools, even less access to informational texts is available (Duke et al., 2003; Moss, 2005). Therefore, supplementary curriculum at the elementary level that is focused on higher level thinking skills with access to engaging informational texts is greatly needed.

With the onset of Common Core State Standards (CCSS) and other curriculum reform initiatives, there has been an increased emphasis on nonfiction reading. Advocates suggest that by fourth grade students should be reading 50% literacy texts and 50% informational texts as part of their repertoire. The number of nonfiction texts to be read increases to 70% of all readings for graduating, college-ready seniors (Calkins, Ehrenworth, & Lehman, 2012). The incorporation of engaging nonfiction texts into an already rigorous reading curriculum is found to motivate students—especially reluctant readers and those with innate curiosity and precocity in a specific content domain. Moreover, the use of nonfiction increases knowledge and access to information beyond the classroom walls and encourages engagement in the practice of becoming lifelong learners (Moss, 2005).

Jacob's Ladder Reading Comprehension Program: Nonfiction (Jacob's Ladder: Nonfiction) is a compilation of the instructional scaffolding and reading exercises necessary to aid students in their journey toward becoming critical and inquisitive readers. Students learn concept development skills through generalizing, predicting and forecasting skills through delineating implications of events/perspectives/situations, comparative analysis skills through discerning textual meaning and author's purpose, and creative analysis skills through synthesizing information and producing new products or ideas (VanTassel-Baska & Stambaugh, 2006a). The questions and tasks for each reading are open-ended, allowing for multiple responses that ultimately improve performance on comprehension tests (Guthrie, Schafer, & Huang, 2001). Progressing through the hierarchy of skills also requires students to reread the text, thereby improving meta-comprehension accuracy (Rawson, Dunlosky, & Thiede, 2000). As many gifted students are able to assimilate information more quickly and make connections within and across disciplines, a comparative analysis of a variety of nonfiction texts supports their development and content acquisition (Rogers, 2007). In addition, the more diverse works students have accessible to read, the more likely they are to show higher achievement gains in addition to reading engagement (Brozo, Shiel, & Topping, 2007).

Introduction to Jacob's Ladder: Nonfiction

Jacob's Ladder: Nonfiction is a supplemental reading program that implements targeted readings adapted primarily from blogs, newspapers, speeches, scientific journals, and biography study. With this program, students engage in an inquiry process that moves from lower order to higher order thinking skills. Starting with basic textual understanding, students learn to critically analyze texts by determining implications and consequences, generalizations, main ideas, vocabulary of the discipline, emotional appeals, and/or creative synthesis. This book is suggested for gifted or high-achieving students in grade 5. It is used to enhance reading comprehension and critical thinking. Tasks are organized into six skill ladders, A–F, and each ladder focuses on a different set of skills. Students "climb" each ladder by answering lower level questions and then moving to higher level questions (or rungs) at the top of each ladder. As many gifted students are more conceptual and prefer whole to part learning (Rogers, 2007), it is also appropriate to begin at the highest rung and scaffold down as needed to ensure that students have mastered the necessary skills. However, each ladder may stand alone as it focuses on a separate critical thinking component in reading. The intent of the ladder design is that students spend more time discussing ideas at the top of the ladder rungs instead of the bottom rungs, although each rung is distinct in its purpose for skill development.

Ladder A focuses on implications and consequences at the highest and most abstract level. By leading students through sequencing and cause-and-effect activities, students learn to draw implications and consequences from readings. Ladder B focuses on making generalizations. Students first learn to provide details and examples and then move to classifying and organizing those details in order to move up to the highest level of making generalizations. Ladder C focuses on themes. Students begin by identifying key literary features or questions about a text and then make inferences about a given textually based situation. Ladder D focuses at the highest level on creative synthesis by leading students through paraphrasing and summarizing activities. Ladder E focuses on students' emotional responses or reactions to the text as well as analyzing emotional appeals that may be evident in some informational readings by distinguishing emotion and fact, and then channeling the information productively. Ladder F provides an emphasis on word choice and vocabulary of the discipline by engaging learners in understanding, applying, and embedding new vocabulary or analyzing appropriate word choice in both their own and others' writing. Ladders are carefully matched to each text based on the key thinking skills that are implicit or explicit within the readings.

Table 1 provides a visual representation of the six ladders and corresponding objectives for each ladder and rung.

Ladder A:
Focus on Implications and Consequences

The goal of Ladder A is to develop prediction and forecasting skills by encouraging students to make connections among the information provided. Starting with sequencing, students learn to recognize basic types of change or sequence of details that occur within a text. Through identifying cause and effect relationships, students then can judge the impact of certain events, perspectives, contexts, or problems. Finally, through recognizing consequences and implications, students predict or analyze positive, negative, or short- and long-term consequences by judging probable outcomes based on data provided. The rungs are as follows:

- **Ladder A, Rung 1, Sequencing:** The lowest rung on the ladder, sequencing, requires students to organize a set of information in order, based on their reading (e.g., List the steps of a recipe in order.).

- **Ladder A, Rung 2, Cause and Effect:** The middle rung, cause and effect, requires students to think about relationships and identify what causes certain effects and/or what effects were brought about because of certain causes (e.g., What causes a cake to rise in the oven? What effect does the addition of egg yolks have on a batter?).

- **Ladder A, Rung 3, Consequences and Implications:** The highest rung on Ladder A requires students to think about both short- and long-term or positive and negative events that may happen as a result of an effect they have identified (e.g., What are the short-

TABLE 1
Goals and Objectives of *Jacob's Ladder Nonfiction Thinking Skills* by Ladder and Rung

	Ladder A	Ladder B	Ladder C	Ladder D	Ladder E	Ladder F
Rung 3	**A3: Consequences and Implications** — Students will be able to explain and predict the short-/long-term or positive/negative implications of an event, problem, solution, perspective, or passage.	**B3: Generalizations** — Students will be able to write and/or justify generalized (conceptual) statements about a reading and/or an idea within or across readings, using data to support their suppositions.	**C3: Theme/Concept** — Students will be able to identify a major idea or theme common throughout the text or series of texts.	**D3: Creative Synthesis** — Students will create something new using what they have learned from the reading (or series of readings) and their synopses.	**E3: Using Emotion** — Students will be able to analyze how emotion affects the passage and/or the reader.	**F3: Playing With Words** — Students will be able to accurately apply strategies to make an argument, express a point, or use domain-specific vocabulary in a different context or their own creation.
Rung 2	**A2: Cause and Effect** — Students will be able to identify relationships between events, contexts, problems, solutions, or other phenomena.	**B2: Classifications** — Students will be able to categorize different aspects of the text or identify and sort categories from a list of topics or details.	**C2: Inference** — Students will be able to use textual clues to make judgments about specific textual events, ideas, or the author's purpose.	**D2: Summarizing** — Students will be able to provide a synopsis of text sections.	**E2: Expressing Emotion** — Students will be able to articulate their feelings about a passage or concept expressed within a passage through a variety of media (e.g., song, art, poem, story, essay, speech).	**F2: Thinking About Words** — Students will be able to analyze the use of words or devices used to craft a message as related to the theme or idea of a text.
Rung 1	**A1: Sequencing** — Students will be able to list, in order of importance or occurrence in the text, specific events or perspectives.	**B1: Details** — Students will be able to list specific details or recall facts related to the text or generate a list of ideas about a specific topic or event given evidence.	**C1: Textual Elements and Understanding** — Students will be able to identify and explain specific elements, such as context, organization, and general understanding of discipline-specific ideas within a given source.	**D1: Paraphrasing** — Students will be able to restate lines read using their own words.	**E1: Understanding Emotion** — Students will be able to explain how emotion and feeling are conveyed in a text and how that may or may not be linked to their personal experience.	**F1: Understanding Words** — Students will be able to identify and define new vocabulary or ideas within the context of a selected passage through the use of context clues.

and long-term consequences of baking at home?). Students learn to draw consequences and implications from the text for application in the real world.

Ladder B: Focus on Generalizations

The goal of Ladder B is to help students develop deductive reasoning skills, moving from concrete elements to abstract ideas. Students begin by learning the importance of concrete details and how they can be organized. By the top rung, students are able to make general statements spanning a topic, discipline, or concept. The rungs are as follows:

- **Ladder B, Rung 1, Details:** The lowest rung on Ladder B, details, requires students to list examples or details from what they have read and/or to list examples they know from the real world or have read about (e.g., Make a list of types of transportation. Write as many as you can think of in 2 minutes.).

- **Ladder B, Rung 2, Classifications:** The middle rung of Ladder B, classifications, focuses on students' ability to categorize examples and details based on characteristics (e.g., How might we categorize the modes of transportation you identified?). This activity builds students' skills in categorization and classification.

- **Ladder B, Rung 3, Generalizations:** The highest rung on Ladder B, generalizations, requires students to use the list and categories generated at Rungs 1 and 2 to develop two to three general statements that apply to *all* of their examples (e.g., Write three true statements about transportation.).

Ladder C: Focus on Themes

The goal of Ladder C is to develop literary analysis skills based on an understanding of literary elements. After completing Ladder C, students state the main themes and ideas of the text after identifying setting, characters, and the context of the piece. The rungs for this ladder are as follows:

- **Ladder C, Rung 1, Textual Elements:** While working on the lowest rung of Ladder C, textual elements, students identify and/or describe the elements, such as the author's purpose or organization of the text. This rung also requires students to develop an understanding of a given perspective, idea, or context (e.g., How does the time period when this piece was written help us understand the purpose?).

- **Ladder C, Rung 2, Inference:** The middle rung of Ladder C, inference, requires students to think through a situation in the text and come to a conclusion based on the information and clues provided (e.g., What evidence exists to suggest that this speech is about the interaction of peace and war?).

- **Ladder C, Rung 3, Theme/Concept:** The highest rung of Ladder C, theme/concept, requires students to determine the central idea or theme of a reading. This exercise necessitates that the students explain an idea from the reading that best states what the text means (e.g., What is the author's perspective on the following statement: "There can be no peace without war"? How are these themes portrayed through the speech? What additional concepts are discussed?).

Ladder D: Focus on Creative Synthesis

The goal of Ladder D is to help students develop skills in creative synthesis in order to foster students' creation of new material based on information from the reading. It moves from the level of restating ideas to creating new ideas or synthesizing multiple ideas into something new about a topic or concept. The rungs are as follows:

- **Ladder D, Rung 1, Paraphrasing:** The lowest rung on Ladder D is paraphrasing. This rung requires students to restate a short passage using their own words (e.g., Explain, in your own words, how a supernova is formed.).

- **Ladder D, Rung 2, Summarizing:** Summarizing, the middle rung on Ladder D, requires students to summarize larger sections of text by selecting the most important key points within the text (e.g., In three sentences or less, summarize the purpose of this news release about supernovas.).

- **Ladder D, Rung 3, Creative Synthesis:** The highest rung on Ladder D requires students to create something new using what they have learned from the reading and their synopses of it (e.g., Create a visual that would complement this news piece and help others better understand the main idea the author is trying to convey.).

Ladder E: Focus on Emotional Development

The goal of Ladder E is to help students develop skills in using their emotional intelligence in order to regulate and modulate behavior with respect to learning and to observe how others use emotional appeal in their writings to evoke emotion. It moves from students' understanding of emotion in self and others, to expressing emotion, to channeling emotion for cognitive ends. There is potential for teachers to use this ladder with many primary source documents—in particular, editorial cartoons and speeches. The rungs are as follows:

- **Ladder E, Rung 1, Understanding Emotion:** The lowest rung on Ladder E focuses on understanding emotion in oneself and others. This requires students to identify emotions in the text and relate them to their own lives (e.g., How did the author of this speech use key scenarios or ideas to evoke emotion?). It also requires them to recognize emotional situations and pinpoint the nature of the emotions involved and what is causing them.

- **Ladder E, Rung 2, Expressing Emotion:** The middle rung on Ladder E, expressing emotion, asks students to express emotion in response to their reading of various selections (e.g., How did this speech appeal to you? How did the author try to appeal to his or her audience? Rewrite the speech in a way that would better appeal to you or others of this time period and include a justification for why you included certain emotional appeals.). Teachers may want to substitute kinesthetic responses in the form of dance or skits that demonstrate an emotional reaction to the selections. Art or music of the day can be great extensions to historical and biographical studies that incorporate this ladder.

- **Ladder E, Rung 3, Using Emotion:** The highest rung on Ladder E, using emotion, encourages students to begin regulating emotion for specific purposes (e.g., Write a letter to the editor expressing your reaction to this excerpt that includes appropriate facts and other compelling evidence and emotional appeals.). In application to nonfiction, students need to demonstrate a clear understanding of how to use emotion effectively for accomplishing specific ends, whether through giving a speech or writing a passionate letter in defense of an idea. The deliberate incorporation of emotion in one's communication is stressed.

Ladder F: Focus on Word Study and Vocabulary of the Discipline

In the Jacob's Ladder: Nonfiction series, Ladder F focuses on word study and vocabulary of the discipline. The goal of Ladder F is to move students from understanding meanings of words to appropriately using words within an applicable context or their own creation.

- **Ladder F, Rung 1, Understanding Words:** The lowest rung on Ladder F focuses on understanding words. It requires students to consider how words are used in the context of the story to promote meaning (e.g., How might you determine what the word *condensation* means through context clues and visual representations provided?). Through textual evidence and informational text features, students find new examples or uses of content-specific words and learn how to recognize and use these words appropriately in other contexts.

- **Ladder F, Rung 2, Thinking About Words:** The middle rung of Ladder F, thinking about words, requires students to think about how the key words or text features studied in the first rung enhance the meaning of the text. Students engage in analyzing author word choice in historical documents or deciphering how to apply new content-specific vocabulary into new situations in scientific articles (e.g., Why did the author choose to use the word *crisis* instead of *tragedy*?).

- **Ladder F, Rung 3, Playing With Words:** The highest rung on Ladder F, playing with words, engages students in reflecting on key words or literary elements and applying them to new situations or contexts. Students are asked to apply the new learning to other writing pieces (e.g., Write your own news blog that teaches second graders about the interaction between condensation and evaporation using what you learned from this text as well as two others that you choose; use new ideas and visuals.), and to select the most important aspects of language or other representations for their own use to meaningfully convey ideas.

Process Skills

Along with the six goals addressed by the ladders, a seventh goal focusing on process skills is incorporated in the Jacob's Ladder curriculum. The aim of this goal is to promote learning through interaction and discussion of reading material in the classroom. After completing the ladders and following guidelines for discussion and teacher feedback, students will be able to:

- articulate their understanding of a text using textual support;

- engage in proper dialogue about the meaning or purpose of a selection, including adding their opinion or perspective, with evidence; and

- discuss varied ideas about the intention of a passage both orally and in writing.

Intended Audience:
Who Should Use Jacob's Ladder

Although the program is targeted for gifted learners and advanced students who need more exposure to higher level thinking skills in reading, the program may be suitable for other learners as well, including those who are twice-exceptional, students from poverty, and those from different cultural backgrounds (VanTassel-Baska & Stambaugh, 2006b). The Jacob's Ladder: Nonfiction series consists of three levels: Grade 3, Grade 4, and Grade 5. (See also the Jacob's Ladder Reading Comprehension Program series, which focuses primarily on fiction sources available for students in grades K–8.) However, teachers may find that they want to vary usage beyond the recommended levels, depending on students' abilities. Evidence suggests that the curriculum can be successfully implemented with gifted and advanced learners as well as other students (Stambaugh, 2007), depending on the level of scaffolding and grade-level choices (e.g., teachers may go up or down a few grade levels based on their students' needs and readiness levels). Thus, the levels vary and overlap to provide opportunities for teachers to select the most appropriate set of readings for meaningful differentiation for their learners' needs.

Organization of Reading Selections

Each nonfiction book contains two main reading sections: nonfiction by discipline and fiction/nonfiction comparative analyses. The nonfiction section includes readings from a variety of disciplines such as mathematics, science, the arts, and social studies. The comparative fiction section pairs poetry readings with companion nonfiction texts such as biography study or a similar/contrasting article that complements the fiction selection in respect to topic or theme. Sometimes, there is another nonfiction piece used for comparison if it represents another type of writing. In addition, within each domain at least one comparative analysis is included. For example, in science, students may read two different nonfiction pieces about a similar phenomenon and answer questions about each piece individually, and then respond to a ladder or question set that compares and contrasts the two pieces. A listing of readings by discipline and ladder appears in Table 2. Care was taken to incorporate readings from multiple perspectives, stakeholders, disciplines, events, time periods, and cultures as available.

Research Base

A quasi-experimental study was conducted using Jacob's Ladder as a supplementary program for grade 3–5 students in Title I schools. After receiving professional development, teachers were instructed to implement the Jacob's Ladder curriculum in addition to their basal reading series and guided reading groups. Nonfiction selections were included as part of this study in addition to poetry and fiction selections.

Findings (N = 495) suggested that when compared to students who used the basal reader only, those students who were exposed to the Jacob's Ladder curriculum showed significant gains in reading comprehension and critical thinking. Likewise, students who used the curriculum showed significant and important growth on curriculum-based assessments that included determining implications and consequences, making inferences, outlining themes and generalizations, and applying creative synthesis. Students reported greater interest in reading and alluded that the curriculum made them "think harder." Teachers reported more in-depth student discussion and personal growth in the ability to ask open-ended questions in reading (Stambaugh, 2007). The same ladders, models, and goals have been applied to this book. An earlier study also documented the growth in reading comprehension and critical thinking that resulted from using the program with gifted students (French, 2006). It is important to note that success of the program and the impact on student achievement occurred under the conditions of ongoing monitoring of program fidelity that included professional development, modeling, and teacher feedback. Thus teachers should try to implement the program as faithfully as possible with respect to its audience and purposes.

TABLE 2
List of Readings and Ladders by Discipline

	Part II: Readings and Student Ladder Sets by Discipline		
Section	**Reading Titles**	**Ladders**	**Comparison Ladder**
Science	Summary of the Clean Air Act	A, D	B
	Flint's Water Crisis	A, C	B
	Four New Elements Added to the Periodic Table	C, D	
	Astronomers Discover Signs of Milky Way's Second-Largest Black Hole	B, C	
	Mindsets: How the Popular Psychological Theory Relates to Success	B	C
	Excerpt From "The Fringe Benefits of Failure and the Importance of Imagination"	B, E	C
Math	How Old Are You—in Seconds?	A	B
	What's the Biggest Number?	C	B
	George Boole and the Wonderful World of 0s and 1s	A, B	
	Focus on the Global Economy	A, D	
Social Studies	Excerpt From "Seeing Red: The Cold War and American Public Opinion"	B, D	
	Excerpt From "Their Finest Hour"	A, B, D	
	Woman's Rights to the Suffrage	A, D	D
	Ain't I a Woman?	B, E	D
The Arts	Excerpt From William Faulkner Nobel Prize Banquet Speech, 1950	A, C	C, D
	Excerpt From Mario Vargas Llosa Nobel Prize Banquet Speech, 2010	A, C	C, D
	Remains of the Past: Roman Art and Architecture	A, B	
	Jacob Lawrence	B, C	
	Duke Ellington	A, D	
	Part III: Readings and Student Ladder Sets for Fiction and Nonfiction Comparisons		
Section	**Reading Titles**	**Ladders**	**Comparison Ladder**
Fiction and Nonfiction Comparison	Break, Break, Break Korean War Photo Analysis	D, F C	E
	Composed Upon Westminster Bridge, September 3, 1802 William Wordsworth	C, F A	C
	At the Window D. H. Lawrence	A C	B
	Bond and Free The Importance of Critical Thinking	C, D A, B, D	C
	The World Is Too Much With Us Should Schools Replace Textbooks With Tablets?	C, F B, D	C

Implementation Considerations

Teachers need to consider certain issues when implementing the Jacob's Ladder curriculum. Because modeling, coaching, and feedback appear to enhance student growth in reading and writing (Pressley et al., 2001; Taylor, Peterson, Pearson, & Rodriguez, 2002), it is recommended that teachers review how to complete the task ladders with the entire class at least once, outlining expectations as well as modeling the process prior to assigning small-group or independent work. As students gain more confidence in the curriculum, teachers should allow more independent work coupled with small-group or paired discussion, and then whole-group sharing with teacher feedback. Jacob's Ladder is *not* intended to be used as a set of worksheets or individual tasks, but rather for the facilitation of ongoing discussion and reasoning among groups of learners from dyads to whole-class discussion groups. The material was designed, however, for advanced readers who can independently read the material and comprehend it. It may be the case that, after trying it with the whole class, there needs to be a fallback position to using it only with a small group who needs accelerated resources and scaffolding.

Completing these activities in dyads or small groups will facilitate discussions that stress collaborative reasoning, thereby fostering greater engagement and higher level thinking (Chin, Anderson, & Waggoner, 2001; Harvey, 2002; Pressley et al., 2001; Taylor et al., 2002). The readings and accompanying ladder questions and activities may be organized into a reading center in the classroom or utilized with reading groups during guided reading for those students who need extensions or substitutions to the regular curriculum. Teachers may also choose to read the selections aloud to students in advanced-level reading groups or to the entire class and solicit responses through methods like think-pair-share, whole-group class discussion, or small-group/individual assignments to be completed prior to engaging in a reading group.

Process of Jacob's Ladder

The process of inquiry and feedback, as led and modeled by the teacher, is critical to the success of the program and student mastery of process skills. Teachers need to solicit multiple student responses and encourage dialogue about various perspectives and interpretations of a given text, requiring students to justify their answers with textual support and concrete examples (VanTassel-Baska & Stambaugh, 2006a, 2006b). Sample follow-up questions for helping students engage in discussion such as those listed on page 14 can be used by the teacher and posted in the classroom to guide students' dialogue. These questions in no way substitute for advanced, content-specific questions nor do they insinuate that there are no "correct" answers. The purpose of teaching these stems encourages students to engage in dialogue and Socratic seminars while being good consumers of text instead of passive listeners who do not move beyond the basic information within a text.

- That's interesting; does anyone have a **different idea**?
- What in the text provides **evidence** for your thinking?
- What do you think the author **means** by . . . ?
- What do you think are the **implications or consequences** of . . . ?
- Does anyone have a different **point of view**? Justify your answer.
- Tell me more about **why** . . .
- Do you notice any **key words** that might be significant? Why?
- How does this text help us **better understand** . . . ?
- I **agree/disagree** with . . . **because** . . .

Beck and McKeown (1998) suggested that academic discourse in reading promotes textual understanding. They recommended guiding students through the text by showing them how to *mark key words* in a text both on their own and as part of whole-group modeling. Teachers are also encouraged to *reframe student responses* in order to ensure that students have a clear voice that is heard and acknowledged as important to understanding. Knowing that teacher stance is critical to the process of reasoning and understanding, teachers are encouraged to help students use evidence from the text to justify responses, including *turning back in the text* to show where ideas were found. Teachers should also *model* metacognitive approaches by thinking aloud about how one may go about developing an idea or comment, *providing annotations* or background information as necessary, and then *synthesizing key ideas* expressed during a discussion. This guidance will promote critical thinking when combined with the discourse of also asking targeted, open-ended questions to help students gain understanding for themselves without being told what to think.

In order for students to maximize their understanding and engagement in reading nonfiction texts, they must see nonfiction as a way to answer their own questions or appeal to their curious nature (Harvey, 2002; Moss & Hendershot, 2002). Some of the challenges when implementing nonfiction reading selections into the curriculum include finding information that is just right for student engagement (i.e., not too hard or not written in a way that does not allow for engagement and understanding), allowing students to have some choice in the types of informational texts or topics they read, and finding time to allow students to investigate and learn new information (Calkins et al., 2012). Allowing students choice in their reading selections and encouraging students to find ways to answer their own questions has been shown to promote engagement, motivation, and more reading of nonfiction texts for all students (Moss & Hendershot, 2002). The Jacob's Ladder nonfiction texts have been selected to complement the general curriculum and to engage students in reading selections that encourage their higher level thinking and broaden their knowledge of information in a variety of disciplines.

For gifted students and other high-ability learners, the process of curriculum compacting allows for students to test out of basic skills and then work on topics of interest. Teachers may compact certain areas of the curriculum and engage students in posing their own questions. Teachers may match student questions to passages within the Jacob's Ladder text or other nonfiction texts, using the ladder framework. The texts do not need to be used in order but may be mixed or matched to student interests and needs. Of course, the curriculum may also be used to teach students how to read and analyze informational texts as they engage in their own line of inquiry.

Grouping and Jacob's Ladder

Jacob's Ladder may be used in a number of different grouping patterns. The program should be introduced initially as a whole-group activity directed by the teacher with appropriate open-ended questions, feedback, and monitoring. After students have examined each type of ladder with teacher guidance, they should be encouraged to use the program by listing key ideas/thoughts independently (not writing out full sentences or paragraphs for each rung), sharing with a partner, and then discussing their findings with a group as part of eliciting different perspectives. The dyad approach provides maximum opportunities for student discussion of the readings and collaborative decisions about the answers to questions posed. One purpose of the program is to solicit meaningful discussion of the text, which is best accomplished in small groups of students at similar reading levels (VanTassel-Baska & Little, 2017). Meta-analyses of the research on grouping practices continue to support instructional grouping in reading as an important part of successful implementation of a reading program for gifted and high-ability learners (Rogers, 2002, 2007).

Demonstrating Growth: Pre- and Postassessments and Student Products

The pre- and postassessments included in Appendix A were designed as a diagnostic-prescriptive approach to guide program implementation of Jacob's Ladder. The pretest should be administered, scored, and then used to guide student instruction and the selection of readings for varied ability groups. Both assessments and the scoring rubric are included in Appendix A.

In both the pre- and postassessments, students read a short passage and respond to the three questions. Question 1 focuses on understanding implications and consequences of the text. Question 2 assesses students' knowledge of key ideas. Question 3 examines students' ability to make connections and inferences provided in the text, and Question 4 measures students' ability to synthesize information acquired. Jacob's Ladder: Nonfiction, Grade 5 incorporates a preassessment and a postassessment using historical speeches as the selected reading.

Upon conclusion of the program or as a midpoint check, the postassessment may be administered to compare to the preassessment results and to measure growth in students' responses. These pre-post results may be used as part of a student portfolio, in a parent-teacher conference, or as documentation of curriculum effectiveness and student progress.

Record-keeping sheets for differentiation within the class are provided in Appendix B. On these forms, teachers record student progress on a 3-point scale: 3 (*applies skills very effectively*), 2 (*understands and applies skills*), or a 1 (*needs more practice with the given skill set*) across readings and ladder sets. These forms may be used as part of a diagnostic/prescriptive approach for selecting more reading materials and ladders based on student understanding or the need for more practice. After teachers administer the preassessment, they may select readings commensurate with key ladder skills needed by individual students and then flexibly group those students according to their levels of understanding of a particular thinking skill. Other forms in Appendix B include blank ladder rungs for students to jot down their answers in preparation for group discussion and metacognitive reflection sheets. The blank ladder rungs for recording answers are not to be used as worksheets that require full sentence responses, but instead as an organizer of thinking or quick outline/bullet points of what students choose to discuss in small or whole-group debriefing. The metacognitive reflection sheets may be used periodically throughout the program as a way for students to monitor their own growth in thinking and to reflect upon the Jacob's Ladder thinking processes.

Grading and Monitoring Student Understanding

Teachers will want to check student answers as ladder segments are completed and conduct an individual or small-group consultation, similar to a writers' workshop format, to ensure that students understand why their answers may be effective or ineffective. In order to analyze student responses and progress across the program, teachers need to monitor student performance, providing specific comments about student work to promote growth and understanding of content. However, the program was *not* intended for students to write down their ideas to every question. Part of the richness of the program comes in student discussions and interactions with the teacher who models key ideas and strategies.

Grading the ladders and responses is at the teacher's discretion. Teachers should not overemphasize the lower rungs in graded activities. Lower rungs are intended partially as a vehicle to the higher level questions at the top of the ladder, as well as a thematic thread for the question clusters created. Top-rung questions may be used as a journal prompt or as part of a graded open-ended writing response. Grades also could be given based on guided discussion after students are familiar with the processes and acceptable responses with evidence. Most of the higher level rung questions, products, and activities can be used for grading. Other rungs may be used that way as well, depending on the thinking required and the task demand.

Time Allotment

Although the time needed to complete Jacob's Ladder tasks will vary by student, most lessons should take students 15–30 minutes to read the selection aloud or with a partner and another 20–30 minutes to complete one ladder individually. More time is required for paired student and whole-group discussion of the questions or for specific creative synthesis tasks that involve more writing or researching. Teachers may wish to set aside 2–3 days each week for focusing on one Jacob's Ladder reading and commensurate ladders, especially when introducing the program. When first starting out with the program, teachers have reported reading and discussing two ladders taking up to a week. As students become more familiar with the process, the timing will vary based on student groupings, the length of the text, the specific questions and products to be completed, the number of ladders used, and student interest in the topic. It is important in introducing the program to select a reading and follow-up ladder work that could be completed in a period in order to model what the program intends.

Alignment to Common Core State Standards in English Language Arts

The new Common Core State Standards are K–12 content standards, developed in math and language arts to illustrate the curriculum emphases needed to develop in all students the skills and concepts needed for the 21st century. Adopted or adapted by many states to date, the standards are organized into key content strands and articulated across all years of schooling. The initiative has been state-based and collaboratively led through two consortia and coordinated by the National Governors Association (NGA) and the Council of Chief State School Officers (CCSSO). Designed by teachers, administrators, and content experts, the standards seek to prepare K–12 students for college and the workplace.

The new standards in language arts are evidence-based, aligned with expectations for success in college and the workplace, and informed by the successes and failures of the current standards and international competition demands. They stress rigor, depth, clarity, and coherence, drawing from key national and international reports in mathematics and science. They provide a framework for curriculum development work that remains to be done—although many states are already engaged in this ongoing process.

Alignment Approaches to the Jacob's Ladder Reading Comprehension Program

Jacob's Ladder exemplifies a model curriculum that addresses the Common Core State Standards in English language arts—with informational texts spanning all content areas—through several approaches, including advanced readings, the use of higher level skills and product demands that address the Common Core emphases for argument and persuasion directly, and a focus on concept/theme development that is mirrored in the new standards.

There are three major strategies the authors of Jacob's Ladder: Nonfiction have used to accomplish the alignment to the Common Core State Standards and advanced instruction that goes beyond typical standards expected of all students.

- Jacob's Ladder provides pathways to advance the learning of the Common Core State Standards for gifted learners. Some of the standards do address higher level skills and concepts that should receive focus throughout the years of schooling, such as a major emphasis on the skills of argument in language arts. However, there are also more discrete skills that may be clustered across grade levels and compressed around higher level skills and concepts for more efficient mastery by the gifted. The Jacob's Ladder curriculum series moves students from lower order comprehension skills in reading to higher order critical reading and thinking skills within the same set of activities, thus advancing their higher level learning in verbal areas.

- The program provides differentiated task demands to address specific Common Core State Standards, and these cut across multiple disciplines but are embedded within contextual analysis and understanding of informational texts across multiple disciplines.

- Standards, such as the reading information text standard in the new Common Core English language arts standards, lend themselves to differentiated interpretation by demonstrating what a typical learner might be able to do at a given stage of development versus what a gifted learner might be able to do (Hughes, Kettler, Shaunessy-Dedrick, & VanTassel-Baska, 2014; VanTassel-Baska, 2013). The differentiated ladder examples in Jacob's Ladder: Nonfiction also show greater complexity, depth, and creativity, using a more advanced curriculum base.

Teachers and administrators are encouraged to align their standards to the different rungs of Jacob's Ladder. This exercise allows educators to see visually which ladders may need more emphasis, based on a curriculum standard, and also to see where the highest leveled rungs of Jacob's Ladder may not be emphasized as much for most learners. However, they are a necessary component for stretching student thinking and differentiating for those who are ready for higher level skills. A chart is included in Appendix C to identify the connections to the CCSS standards of the ladder selections in this book.

Because English language arts standards can be grouped together in application, much of the project work in Jacob's Ladder connects to the new Common Core State Standards and shows how multiple standards can be addressed across content areas. For example, research projects are designed to address the research standard in English language arts by delineating a product demand for research on an issue, beginning by asking researchable questions and using multiple sources to answer them, and then representing the findings in tables, graphs, and other visual displays that are explained in the text and presented to an audience with implications for a plan of action. This approach to interdisciplinary work across math, science, and fictional texts is a central part of the Jacob's Ladder: Nonfiction program.

References

Beck, I. L., & McKeown, M. G. (1998). Comprehension: The sine qua non of reading. In S. Patton & M. Holmes (Eds.), *The keys to literacy* (pp. 40–52). Washington, DC: Council for Basic Education.

Bransford, J. D., Brown, A. L., & Cocking, R. R. (2000). *How people learn: Brain, mind, experience.* Washington, DC: National Academy Press.

Brozo, W., Shiel, G., & Topping, K. (2007). Engagement in reading: Lessons learned from three PISA countries. *Journal of Adolescent and Adult Literacy, 51,* 304–315.

Calkins, L., Ehrenworth, M., & Lehman, C. (2012). *Pathways to the Common Core: Accelerating achievement.* Portsmouth, NH: Heinemann.

Chin, C. A., Anderson, R. C., & Waggoner, M. A. (2001). Patterns of discourse in two kinds of literature discussion. *Reading Research Quarterly, 30,* 378–411.

Duke, N. K., Bennett-Armistead, V. S., & Roberts, E. M. (2003). Filling the great void: Why we should bring nonfiction into the early-grade classroom. *American Educator, 27,* 30–35.

French, H. (2006). *The use of Jacob's Ladder to enhance critical thinking abilities in gifted and promising learner populations* (Unpublished doctoral dissertation). William & Mary, Williamsburg, VA.

Guthrie, J. T., Schafer, W. D., & Huang, C. (2001). Benefits of opportunity to read and balanced instruction on the NAEP. *Journal of Educational Research, 94,* 145–162.

Harvey, S. (2002). Nonfiction inquiry: Using real reading and writing to explore the world. *Language Arts, 80,* 12–22.

Hughes, C. E., Kettler, T., Shaunessy-Dedrick, E., & VanTassel-Baska, J. (2014). *A teacher's guide to using the Common Core State Standards with gifted and advanced learners in the English language arts.* Waco, TX: Prufrock Press.

Moss, B. (2005). Making a case and a place for effective content area literacy instruction in the elementary grades. *The Reading Teacher, 59,* 46–55.

Moss, B., & Hendershot, J. (2002). Exploring sixth graders' selection of nonfiction trade books. *The Reading Teacher, 56,* 6–17.

Pressley, M., Wharton-McDonald, R., Allington, R., Block, C. C., Morrow, L., Tracey, D., . . . Woo, D. (2001). A study of effective first-grade literacy instruction. *Scientific Studies of Reading, 5,* 35–58.

Rawson, K. A., Dunlosky, J., & Thiede, K. W. (2000). The rereading effect: Metacomprehension accuracy improves across reading trials. *Memory & Cognition, 28*(6), 1004.

Rogers, K. (2002). *Re-forming gifted education: How parents and teachers can match the program to the child.* Scottsdale, AZ: Great Potential Press.

Rogers, K. B. (2007). Lessons learned about educating the gifted and talented: A synthesis of the research on educational practice. *Gifted Child Quarterly, 51,* 382–396.

Stambaugh, T. (2007). *Effects of the Jacob's Ladder Reading Comprehension Program* (Unpublished doctoral dissertation). William & Mary, Williamsburg, VA.

Taylor, B. M., Pearson, P. D., Peterson, D. S., & Rodriguez, M. C. (2003). Reading growth in high-poverty classrooms: The influence of teacher practices that encourage cognitive engagement in literacy learning. *The Elementary School Journal, 104,* 3–30.

Taylor, B. M., Peterson, D. S., Pearson, P. D., & Rodriguez, M. C. (2002). Looking inside classrooms: Reflecting on the "how" as well as the "what" in effective reading instruction. *Reading Teacher, 56,* 270–279.

Tivnan, T., & Hemphill, L. (2005). Comparing four literacy reform models in high-poverty schools: Patterns of first-grade achievement. *Elementary School Journal, 105,* 419–443.

VanTassel-Baska, J. (2013). *Using the Common Core State Standards for English language arts with gifted and advanced learners.* Waco, TX: Prufrock Press.

VanTassel-Baska, J., & Stambaugh, T. (2006a). *Comprehensive curriculum for gifted learners* (3rd ed.). Needham Heights, MA: Allyn & Bacon.

VanTassel-Baska, J., & Stambaugh, T. (2006b). Project Athena: A pathway to advanced literacy development for children of poverty. *Gifted Child Today, 29*(2), 58–65.

VanTassel-Baska, J., & Little, C. (Eds.). (2016). *Content-based curriculum for gifted learners* (2nd ed.). Waco, TX: Prufrock Press.

Villaume, S. K., & Brabham, E. G. (2002). Comprehension instruction: Beyond strategies. *The Reading Teacher, 55,* 672–676.

Part II: Readings and Student Ladder Sets by Discipline

Science

Section 1 includes the selected readings and accompanying question sets for each science selection. Each reading is followed by one or two sets of questions; each set is aligned to one of the six ladder skills. The ladder skills covered by each selection are as follows:

Reading Titles	Ladders	Comparison Ladder
Summary of the Clean Air Act	A, D	B
Flint's Water Crisis	A, C	B
Four New Elements Added to the Periodic Table	C, D	
Astronomers Discover Signs of Milky Way's Second-Largest Black Hole	B, C	
Mindsets: How the Popular Psychological Theory Relates to Success	B	C
Excerpt From "The Fringe Benefits of Failure and the Importance of Imagination"	B, E	C

Summary of the Clean Air Act

The Clean Air Act (CAA) is the comprehensive federal law that regulates air emissions from stationary and mobile sources. Among other things, this law authorizes EPA [Environmental Protection Acency] to establish National Ambient Air Quality Standards (NAAQS) to protect public health and public welfare and to regulate emissions of hazardous air pollutants.

One of the goals of the Act was to set and achieve NAAQS in every state by 1975 in order to address the public health and welfare risks posed by certain widespread air pollutants. The setting of these pollutant standards was coupled with directing the states to develop state implementation plans (SIPs), applicable to appropriate industrial sources in the state, in order to achieve these standards. The Act was amended in 1977 and 1990 primarily to set new goals (dates) for achieving attainment of NAAQS since many areas of the country had failed to meet the deadlines.

Section 112 of the Clean Air Act addresses emissions of hazardous air pollutants. Prior to 1990, CAA established a risk-based program under which only a few standards were developed. The 1990 Clean Air Act Amendments revised Section 112 to first require issuance of technology-based standards for major sources and certain area sources. "Major sources" are defined as a stationary source or group of stationary sources that emit or have the potential to emit 10 tons per year or more of a hazardous air pollutant or 25 tons per year or more of a combination of hazardous air pollutants. An "area source" is any stationary source that is not a major source.

For major sources, Section 112 requires that EPA establish emission standards that require the maximum degree of reduction in emissions of hazardous air pollutants. These emission standards are commonly referred to as "maximum achievable control technology" or "MACT" standards. Eight years after the technology-based MACT standards are issued for a source category, EPA is required to review those standards to determine whether any residual risk exists for that source category and, if necessary, revise the standards to address such risk.

Reference

United States Environmental Protection Agency. (2015). *Summary of the Clean Air Act*. Retrieved from https://www.epa.gov/laws-regulations/summary-clean-air-act

A3

Consequences and Implications

What are the positive and negative implications of the Clean Air Act for changing American lifestyles? Cite examples from the Act to support your idea.

A2

Cause and Effect

What causes polluted air? What are its effects?

A1

Sequencing

What are the top five most important details to identify in the Clean Air Act? Why are these significant?

Creative Synthesis

Create an act of your own that would seek to control a harmful substance on human living conditions. Provide the following sections:

- In your first paragraph, define what it is that is harmful and state your goals.
- In the second paragraph, cite what actions would be taken to control the harmful substance.
- In the third paragraph, cite the parameters of control—time limits, amounts of the substance allowed, and other considerations.
- In the last paragraph, provide information on how the law would be reviewed to see if it is working and being applied.
- Brainstorm ways that your written act could be improved, and brought forward for consideration.

Summarizing

Summarize your understanding of the power of the Act. Provide evidence to support your points.

Paraphrasing

Paraphrase the last paragraph of the passage.

D3

D2

D1

SUMMARY OF THE CLEAN AIR ACT

Flint's Water Crisis

Have you ever thought about the water that comes from your sink? It's safe, right? Americans take for granted that the water pouring from their faucets is clean enough to drink, but residents of Flint, MI, are living with a new reality after investigations found dangerous levels of lead in the water supply, causing the city's mayor, Michigan's governor, and President Obama to declare a state of emergency for the city.

The crisis began in April 2014, when Michigan temporarily switched the city's drinking water source from Lake Huron to the Flint River in an effort to save money while a new pipeline connecting Flint to the lake was under construction. Residents noticed soon after that the water was dirty, tasted funny, and even smelled bad.

One resident, Lee-Anne Walters, contacted the U.S. Environmental Protection Agency (EPA) with concerns about dark sediment floating in her water, which she feared was making her children sick. In February 2015, the EPA notified the Michigan Department of Environmental Quality that it found the water in Walters's home had 104 parts per billion (ppb) of lead, nearly seven times greater than the EPA limit of 15 ppb.

Later that spring, scientists from Virginia Tech came to Flint to investigate the problem, testing the water in 271 homes and finding lead levels in the water so high in some cases that it met the criteria for "toxic waste" as defined by the EPA. The water in Flint homes tested as high as 13,200 ppb. The EPA's threshold for being considered hazardous waste is 5,000 ppb.

Lead contamination can cause harmful health effects in animals and humans, especially kids, who can experience a variety of long-term health issues if they have too much lead in their blood. These include hearing problems, developmental delays, slower growth, behavior and learning problems, fatigue, vomiting, stomach pain, and irritability. Since the crisis began, estimates suggest that the proportion of Flint's children with above-average levels of lead in their blood has nearly doubled. Anyone with too much lead in his or her blood can experience impacts to the functioning of his or her heart, kidneys, and nerves.

One question that arose related to the crisis was how so much lead made it into the water supply. Investigations found that the water in the Flint River was highly corrosive—able to break down materials through chemical reactions—and needed to be treated with an anti-corrosive agent before it could be considered a safe source for drinking water. (How corrosive was it? Experts found it to be 19 times more corrosive than the water in another Michigan city, Detroit, which also gets its water from Lake Huron.) But the state's Department of Environmental Quality didn't take this action (breaking a federal law in the process), which led to the corrosive water being sent to homes, where it ate away at the pipes that carried it. Approximately half of those pipes were made of lead, which then made its way into the water.

Even though Flint switched its water supply back to Lake Huron in October 2015, the damage was done—the corrosion in the pipes is still causing unusually high levels of lead in the city's tap water. Flint's water is now thought to be safe for bathing, but not drinking, meaning its 100,000 residents must depend on bottled water and water filters. Because 41.6% of the city's residents live below the poverty line, they are largely relying on donations of these items to help them have safe water to drink. Many residents are suffering from health issues as a result of the lead poisoning and other toxins being released into the water.

Investigations about what happened—and who's to blame—are still ongoing, with class action lawsuits being filed and various reforms underway. An independent panel has found "governmental failure" and "inaction and environmental injustice," according to *The New York Times*, concluding that "disregard for the concerns of poor and minority people contributed to the government's slow response to complaints from residents of Flint, Mich., about the foul and discolored water that was making them sick."

References

Bosman, J. (2016). Flint water crisis inquiry finds state ignored warning signs. *The New York Times*. Retrieved from http://www.nytimes.com/2016/03/24/us/flint-water-crisis.html?_r=0

CNN Library. (2016). *Flint water crisis fast facts*. Retrieved from http://www.cnn.com/2016/03/04/us/flint-water-crisis-fast-facts/

Walters, J. M. (2016). Flint's water crisis. *Science World*. Retrieved from http://scienceworld.scholastic.com/Chemistry-News/2016/01/Flint-s-Water-Crisis

Consequences and Implications

A3

What will be the consequences of the problem in the next several months? What are the long-term consequences of the problem for Flint? For other communities?

Cause and Effect

A2

What was the cause of the water problem as you can discern from the article? What impact did it have on the community?

Sequencing

A1

In the article you just read, what was the sequence of events leading to the discovery of the problem with the water in Flint, MI?

FLINT'S WATER CRISIS

Theme/Concept

C3

Create a different headline for the article based on your analysis of the purpose of this text.

Inference

C2

What has been and is yet to be done to solve the water crisis?

Textual Elements and Understanding

C1

What are the main problems listed in this article?

FLINT'S WATER CRISIS

Comparison Ladder for "Summary of the Clean Air Act" and "Flint's Water Crisis"

Of the two readings just completed, both are concerned about public welfare, one in respect to air and one in respect to water. The following ladder provides students the opportunity to analyze these two nonfiction selections as a pair.

Name: _____ Date: _____

Generalizations

B3

Write at least three generalizations about the government's role in keeping people safe that would be true of both air and water in the U.S.

Classifications

B2

How would you categorize the effectiveness of each piece in meeting its intended purpose?

Details

B1

What are the similarities and differences of the purposes of the two readings? Cite specific details.

Four New Elements Added to the Periodic Table

Does your science book contain a copy of the periodic table? If so, there's a good chance it's no longer correct.

In January 2016, scientists confirmed the discovery of four new elements, numbers 113, 115, 117, and 118—the first to be added to the periodic table since 2011. The new additions fill out the seventh row of the table, which organizes all of the currently known elements by their properties.

Three of the elements came out of a collaborative effort by scientists from the Joint Institute for Nuclear Research in Dubna, Russia, and the Lawrence Livermore National Laboratory in California. The fourth, 113, was discovered by the Riken Institute in Japan and is the first-ever element found by researchers in Asia.

The elements will later be named by their scientists according to classifications set by the International Union of Pure and Applied Chemistry (IUPAC): "New elements can be named after a mythological concept, a mineral, a place or country, a property, or a scientist."

Each of the four new elements represents what scientists classify as "superheavy" elements—a designation given to those with more than 104 protons. An element's atomic number equals the number of protons, or positively charged particles, in the nucleus (center) of one of its atoms. The atomic number designates its place on the periodic table; in this case, the elements had 113, 115, 117, and 118 protons.

Superheavy elements cannot be found in nature, but are created synthetically by using particle accelerators to smash atoms of different elements into each other and track the following decay of the radioactive superheavy elements. As with other superheavy elements at the end of the periodic table, the four new elements only exist for fractions of a second before decaying into other elements.

Even though the elements are synthetic, they create greater possibilities for scientists to learn more about the chemical elements around us.

"Filling in the seventh row of the periodic table is a great big deal to us chemists because it expands what we know about nature; these elements really do exist," Mark Cesa, president of the IUPAC, told the *Chicago Tribune*. "It tells us even more new elements may be possible."

The elements' discovery also opens the door to scientists seeking out newer, even heavier elements—hoping to find an element or group of elements that are both stable and useful. Along the way, scientists learn more and more about how atoms are held together.

And students get to see how chemistry can be exciting, ever-changing, and full of potential discoveries. Chicago-area chemistry professor Jeff Jankowski urges his students to consider the technology behind the research and look beyond the challenges of making such new elements: "It's the journey. It's not the destination, I tell students."

As he told the *Chicago Tribune*, "if scientists can detect elements that have such short lives, think of what they can do in other fields. Maybe we will be able to detect disease earlier."

References

Baker, S. (2016). Chemistry community reacts to filling gaps in periodic table. *Chicago Tribune*. Retrieved from http://www.chicagotribune.com/suburbs/naperville-sun/news/ct-nvs-naperville-new-elements-st-0108-20160112-story.html

Chappell, B. (2016). 4 new elements are added to the periodic table. *NPR*. Retrieved from http://www.npr.org/sections/thetwo-way/2016/01/04/461904077/4-new-elements-are-added-to-the-periodic-table

Guardian staff. (2016). Periodic table's seventh row finally filled in as four new elements are added. *The Guardian*. Retrieved from http://www.theguardian.com/science/2016/jan/04/periodic-tables-seventh-row-finally-filled-as-four-new-elements-are-added

Walters, J. M. (2016). Four new elements discovered. *ScienceWorld*. Retrieved from http://scienceworld.scholastic.com/Chemistry-News/2016/01/four-new-elements-discovered

Name: _____ Date: _____

Theme/Concept

C3

Why is this discovery important?

Inference

C2

Are there any superheavy elements in the periodic table now? What can you infer about how the periodic table is organized, based on the article information?

Textual Elements and Understanding

C1

Why are some elements known as being "superheavy"?

FOUR NEW ELEMENTS ADDED TO THE PERIODIC TABLE

D3

Creative Synthesis

Create a new name for each element, based on the rules found in the fourth paragraph. Justify your choices by using scientific evidence from this article to support your selections.

D2

Summarizing

Summarize the nature of the discovery made for future innovation.

D1

Paraphrasing

Paraphrase the scientists' reaction to the discovery.

FOUR NEW ELEMENTS ADDED TO THE PERIODIC TABLE

Name: _____ Date: _____

Astronomers Discover Signs of Milky Way's Second Largest Black Hole

Astronomers in Japan recently detected signs of the first-ever intermediate mass black hole in the Milky Way—a discovery that may be the key to understanding the birth of supermassive black holes located in the centers of galaxies.

Using two radio telescopes (the Nobeyama 45-m Telescope in Japan and the ASTE Telescope in Chile, both operated by the National Astronomical Observatory [NAOJ] in Japan), a team of astronomers led by Tomoharu Oka observed an enigmatic gas cloud orbiting only 200 light years from the center of the Milky Way, detailing their findings in a January 2016 report. Oka's team say the gas cloud, labeled CO-0.40-0.22, may have been flung about by an intermediate mass black hole with a mass of 100,000 times the mass of our sun.

What makes the gas cloud the researchers found so unusual is its surprisingly wide velocity dispersion. The cloud contains gas with a very wide range of speeds. Results show the cloud has an elliptical shape and consists of two components: (1) a compact, but low density component with a very wide velocity dispersion of 100 km/s, and (2) a dense component extending 10 light years with a narrow velocity dispersion.

As the NAOJ explained on its website, what makes the velocity dispersion so wide is the lack of holes inside the cloud. Additionally, when the scientists probed the details of the cloud with X-ray and infrared observations, no compact objects were found.

The team then performed a simple computer simulation of gas clouds flung by a strong gravity source. The researchers found that a hypothetical gravity source with 100,000 times the mass of the sun, inside an area with a radius of 0.3 light years, provided the best fit to the observed data.

"Considering the fact that no compact objects are seen in X-ray or infrared observations," Oka said, "as far as we know, the best candidate for the massive object is a black hole."

How can the discovery shed light on how other black holes are formed?

Astronomers already know about two types of black holes. Stellar-mass black holes, whose masses can range from about five times to tens of times the mass of our sun, are believed to form in supernova explosions. Supermassive black holes, which are thought to lie at the center of the Milky Way and countless other galaxies, have masses ranging from several million to billions of times the mass of our sun. Scientists do not know how supermassive black holes are formed.

One theory, however, is that supermassive black holes are created from the merging of many intermediate mass black holes—a concept conceived by scientists even though none of these holes had previously been found.

This discovery opens the doors for new ways of searching for black holes with radio telescopes. Other gas clouds similar to CO-0.40-0.22 have been observed. Oka's team proposed that some of these clouds might also contain black holes.

Black holes are difficult to find—although a study suggested there are 100 million black holes in the Milky Way, X-ray observations have only found dozens of these. Most black holes may be "dark" and difficult to see. Oka hopes his team's discovery can change that, suggesting that, "Investigations of gas motion with radio telescopes may provide a complementary way to search for dark black holes."

As he added, observing the Milky Way and other nearby galaxies using radio telescopes may "have the potential to increase the number of black hole candidates dramatically."

References

Byrd, D. (2016). Milky Way's second-largest black hole? *EarthSky*. Retrieved from http://earthsky.org/space/milky-ways-second-largest-black-hole

National Astronomical Observatory of Japan. (2016). *Signs of second largest black hole in the Milky Way—Possible missing link in black hole evolution*. Retrieved from http://www.nao.ac.jp/en/news/science/2016/20160115-nro.html

Signs of second largest black hole in the Milky Way. (2016). *Astronomy Magazine*. Retrieved from http://www.astronomy.com/news/2016/01/signs-of-second-largest-black-hole-in-the-milky-way

Generalizations

B3

Create three generalizations about black holes, based on the reading.

Classifications

B2

Create at least three section headings for this article (other than "introduction" and "conclusion") based on the information presented. What are your three headings and what was your rationale for each?

Details

B1

What details do you wish the author would have provided but were not included about black holes and this discovery? Why do you think that information was missing? Should this information have been included? Why or why not?

ASTRONOMERS DISCOVER SIGNS OF MILKY WAY'S SECOND LARGEST BLACK HOLE

Theme/Concept

C3

Visuals can be very important when helping readers understand text. Design a visual to summarize this article or a section of it that would help readers better understand the content.

Inference

C2

What makes this discovery so important, according to the article?

Textual Elements and Understanding

C1

Why do the scientists believe the gas cloud they found is evidence of a black hole? (Include at least six details or reasons.)

ASTRONOMERS DISCOVER SIGNS OF MILKY WAY'S SECOND LARGEST BLACK HOLE

Mindsets: How the Popular Psychological Theory Relates to Success

If someone told you that you had a fixed mindset, what would you think he or she meant? What if he or she told you that you had a growth mindset? These two terms are quickly becoming the biggest buzzwords in psychology, with groups from education, business, and sports adopting the theory that changing one's mindset can change one's successes.

But what does it even mean, mindset? To Stanford psychologist Carol Dweck, we all possess certain ways of thinking about intelligence and achievement in life. If you have a fixed mindset, you believe that intelligence and talent is innate, or fixed. It's something you're born with. If you have a growth mindset, you believe that intelligence and talent can be developed or learned.

In her work with students, Dweck found that how students perceived their abilities played a role in their motivation and achievement. Further, if teachers changed students' perceptions (or mindsets), they could boost these same students' achievements. As Dweck noted in an *Education Week* article,

> More precisely, students who believed their intelligence could be developed (a growth mindset) outperformed those who believed their intelligence was fixed (a fixed mindset). And when students learned through a structured program that they could "grow their brains" and increase their intellectual abilities, they did better. Finally, we found that having children focus on the process that leads to learning (like hard work or trying new strategies) could foster a growth mindset and its benefits.

In developing her theories about mindset, Dweck looked more closely at the concept of failure, wondering why some students gave up after encountering difficulties while others "who were no more skilled continue to strive and learn." She soon discovered her answer: it had to do with people's beliefs about *why* they failed.

Dweck found that when students attributed poor performance to lack of ability rather than lack of effort, they lost motivation. As she discussed in a *Scientific American* article:

In 1972, when I taught a group of elementary and middle school children who displayed helpless behavior in school that a lack of effort (rather than lack of ability) led to their mistakes on math problems, the kids learned to keep trying when the problems got tough. They also solved many more problems even in the face of difficulty. Another group of helpless children who were simply rewarded for their success on easier problems did not improve their ability to solve hard math problems. These experiments were an early indication that a focus on effort can help resolve helplessness and engender success.

Dweck's theories about motivation and failure extend beyond the classroom. She and many others cite multiple examples of famous business people, athletes, and writers, who persevered even in the face of defeat. One of those often cited is J. K. Rowling, who, despite being depressed, on welfare, and a single mother, continued writing her Harry Potter series. And, even after multiple rejections from publishers once her novel was completed, she continued to pursue publication until she received an acceptance. Rowling now boasts an impressive list of best-selling titles, from her adult mystery novels to her wildly popular Harry Potter series.

So, does changing your mindset truly change your chances at success? More studies are underway as the theory continues to gain popularity, but the next time you wonder if putting forth a little more effort could truly boost your performance, give the mindset theory a shot—you might just find adopting a growth mindset is worth it.

References

Dweck, C. (2015). Carol Dweck revisits the "growth mindset." *Education Week*. Retrieved from http://www.edweek.org/ew/articles/2015/09/23/carol-dweck-revisits-the-growth-mindset.html

Dweck, C. S. (2015). The secret to raising smart kids. *Scientific American*. Retrieved from http://www.scientificamerican.com/article/the-secret-to-raising-smart-kids1

Pollock, M. (n.d.). The science of perseverance: How your mindset strengthens or weakens your motivation. Retrieved from http://www.michaeldpollock.com/mindset-motivation-perseverance

Generalizations

B3

Write two generalizations about the impact of mindset on success.

Classifications

B2

Think about times you have had a fixed or growth mindset. Create a T-chart with one column labeled "fixed" and the other column labeled "growth." Provide examples from the text as well as personal examples about how students may act or what they might say when they have a fixed or growth mindset.

Details

B1

What details in the article suggest that a fixed mindset is harmful to success?

MINDSETS: HOW THE POPULAR PSYCHOLOGICAL THEORY RELATES TO SUCCESS

Excerpt From "The Fringe Benefits of Failure and the Importance of Imagination"

J. K. Rowling: Harvard Commencement Address, 2008

What I feared most for myself at your age was not poverty, but failure . . .

However, the fact that you are graduating from Harvard suggests that you are not very well-acquainted with failure. You might be driven by a fear of failure quite as much as a desire for success . . . Ultimately, we all have to decide for ourselves what constitutes failure, but the world is quite eager to give you a set of criteria if you let it. So I think it fair to say that by any conventional measure, a mere seven years after my graduation day, I had failed on an epic scale. An exceptionally short-lived marriage had imploded, and I was jobless, a lone parent, and as poor as it is possible to be in modern Britain, without being homeless. The fears that my parents had had for me, and that I had had for myself, had both come to pass, and by every usual standard, I was the biggest failure I knew.

Now, I am not going to stand here and tell you that failure is fun . . . I had no idea then how far the tunnel extended, and for a long time, any light at the end of it was a hope rather than a reality.

So why do I talk about the benefits of failure? . . . Had I really succeeded at anything else, I might never have found the determination to succeed in the one arena I believed I truly belonged. I was set free, because my greatest fear had been realised, and I was still alive, and I still had a daughter whom I adored, and I had an old typewriter and a big idea . . .

It is impossible to live without failing at something, unless you live so cautiously that you might as well not have lived at all—in which case, you fail by default.

Failure gave me an inner security that I had never attained by passing examinations. Failure taught me things about myself that I could have learned no other way. I discovered that I had a strong will, and more discipline than I had suspected; I also found out that I had friends whose value was truly above the price of rubies . . . You will never truly know yourself, or the strength of your relationships, until both have been tested by adversity. Such knowledge is a true gift . . .

Note. Excerpted from "The Fringe Benefits of Failure, and the Importance of Imagination," by J. K. Rowling, 2008, retrieved from http://news.harvard.edu/gazette/story/2008/06/text-of-j-k-rowling-speech

Generalizations

B3

Write two true statements from the speech about the relationship between success and failure.

Classifications

B2

How does Rowling categorize success? Highlight in the article places where she talks about her definition of success.

Details

B1

What details in the speech suggest what Rowling thinks about failure? Is it positive, negative, or both?

EXCERPT FROM "THE FRINGE BENEFITS OF FAILURE AND THE IMPORTANCE OF IMAGINATION"

Using Emotion

E3

What advice would you give to an older student about success versus failure? Give the advice in an original form such as a rap song, poem, or letter.

Expressing Emotion

E2

Think about a time when you failed. What did you learn? How does what you learned compare to what Rowling learned from her failures?

Understanding Emotion

E1

How did you feel after reading this speech? Why?

EXCERPT FROM "THE FRINGE BENEFITS OF FAILURE AND THE IMPORTANCE OF IMAGINATION"

Comparison Ladder for "Mindsets: How the Popular Psychological Theory Relates to Success" and "Excerpt From 'The Fringe Benefits of Failure and the Importance of Imagination'"

The speech and the article students just read constitute important ideas about how to think about success and failure in life. Each piece provides a different perspective on the issue that is valuable for students to think about and consider as they grow and develop. Students now have the opportunity to analyze the two pieces directly.

Theme/Concept

C3

How is the theme of overcoming failure present in both pieces? Create a concept map to illustrate your thinking about overcoming failure, citing evidence from both articles.

Inference

C2

What would you suggest to someone who has a fixed mindset, based on Rowling's example as well as the mindset theory?

Textual Elements and Understanding

C1

What words or phrases does Rowling use in her speech to suggest that she has a growth mindset? Highlight them and compare your findings with a partner.

COMPARISON LADDER FOR "MINDSETS: HOW THE POPULAR PSYCHOLOGICAL THEORY RELATES TO SUCCESS" AND "EXCERPT FROM 'THE FRINGE BENEFITS OF FAILURE AND THE IMPORTANCE OF IMAGINATION'"

Math

Section 2 includes the selected readings and accompanying question sets for each math selection. Each reading is followed by one or two sets of questions; each set is aligned to one of the six ladder skills. The ladder skills covered by each selection are as follows:

Reading Titles	Ladders	Comparison Ladder
How Old Are You—in Seconds?	A	B
What's the Biggest Number?	C	B
George Boole and the Wonderful World of 0s and 1s	A, B	
Focus on the Global Economy	A, D	

How Old Are You—in Seconds?

by David M. Schwartz

Do you want to be a lot older? Here's how: state your age in seconds instead of years!

Ready to do some math? But what math will you do?

First you have to design a problem-solving strategy. There are many approaches but for all of them, consider that with every passing second, you are a second older. So your age is a moving target. Best to pick a specific time of day and find your age in seconds at that time today.

It doesn't really matter what time of day you pick. If you can find out from your birth certificate what time of day you were born, you could select that time today for your target. If you were born at 4:14 p.m., you will find out how old you are (in seconds) at 4:14 p.m. today.

Or just pick any time today and pretend you were born at that time.

What next? I hope you will try out your own approach but here is a simple strategy that would work:

Step 1. How many days old are you? Figure out how many days elapsed between the day you were born and your most recent birthday. There are 365 days in a year, not counting leap years. In your lifetime, every year divisible by 4 was a leap year and it had a 366th day, which was February 29th. So add an extra day for each February 29th you've lived through.

Then figure out how many days have passed since your last birthday. Try to find a way to make this job quicker than counting each day. Look at calendars as you do this to find shortcuts.

Now you have your age in days. It's already looking like a big number, isn't it? Just wait!

2016
July

Su	Mo	Tu	We	Th	Fr	Sa
					1	2
3	4	5	6	7	8	9
10	11	12	13	14	15	16
17	18	19	20	21	22	23
24	25	26	27	28	29	30
31						

Step 2. How many seconds are in a day? Think about how to figure this out. You know how many seconds are in a minute (60) and how many minutes are in an hour (60) and how many hours are in a day (24). So how many seconds are in a day? Multiply $60 \times 60 \times 24$. Bet you didn't realize a day was so long!

Step 3. So what's Step 3? You now know how many days you have lived and how many seconds are in a day, so what do you do next? Again, multiply!

Next time someone tells you you're not old enough to do something, you can tell him or her, "Oh yes I am. I'm 299,592,620. That's what I was at 11:30 this morning. Now I'm even older!"

Good luck with that!

Consequences and Implications

A3

What does the author explain as the positive consequences of telling someone how old you are in seconds instead of years?

Cause and Effect

A2

What effect does a leap year have on calculating how old you are in days, according to the article?

Sequencing

A1

In your own words, sequence the steps necessary to determine how many days you have lived according to the article. How old are you in days using the steps from the article? Prove you are correct.

HOW OLD ARE YOU—IN SECONDS?

What's the Biggest Number?
by David M. Schwartz

Think of a big number. How about one million? It's a thousand thousand. That's a lot. If you counted nonstop to a million, it would take you about 23 days.

A million is small compared to a billion, which is a thousand million. Want to count that high? You'll be at it for 95 years. But a trillion makes a billion look puny. A trillion is a thousand billion (or a million million). Counting that high would take you 200,000 years. Have fun!

Of course trillion is not the biggest number. There's quadrillion, quintillion, sextillion, septillion, octillion, nonillion, decillion, and more. Each is a thousand of the previous one. There's even a humongous number called vigintillion, a one with 63 zeros.

But vigintillion is a shrimp compared to a googol. Googol? Notice how it's spelled: G-O-O-G-O-L, not G-O-O-G-L-E. The number googol is a one with a hundred zeros. It got its name from a nine-year old boy. A googol is more than all the hairs in the world. It's more than all the grass blades and all the grains of sand. It's even more than the number of atoms in the universe. Astrophysicists estimate the number of atoms to be a one with 72 zeros. You'd need to add 28 more zeros to get to a googol.

Incidentally, a few years ago, the two men who had invented a powerful new internet search engine decided to name their website and company for the gigantic number googol. But they spelled it wrong. That's why the company Google is spelled with an L-E. But the number googol is still spelled with an O-L.

Googol is so large that it's practically useless, but the boy who named it came up with a name for an even bigger number, "googolplex." A googolplex is a one with a googol zeros. There isn't enough ink in all the pens of the world to write that many zeros but feel free to give it a try.

So is googolplex the biggest number? What about a googolplex and one? Two googolplex? A googolplex googolplex? Any number you say, I can say one bigger.

I hear you asking, "What about infinity? Isn't that the biggest number?" Sorry, but infinity isn't a number. A number specifies an amount and infinity is no amount. It means "goes on and on forever."

And that's what numbers do. They go on and on forever. Infinity is not a number but numbers are infinite.

Name: _____ Date: _____

Theme/Concept

C3

Create a concept map that outlines the author's view of infinity.

Inference

C2

What does the author mean when stating that "infinity is not a number but numbers are infinite"?

Textual Elements and Understanding

C1

What is the problem presented in this article? How do you know?

WHAT'S THE BIGGEST NUMBER?

Comparison Ladder for "How Old Are You—in Seconds?" and "What's the Biggest Number?"

The two articles on mathematics provide an interesting pairing of ideas about the use of numbers. Students may now analyze how the articles compare in respect to ideas and messages for the reader.

Generalizations

B3

What do each of the articles suggest about the purpose of using large numbers? Write at least two sentences about numbers that would be true of each article.

Classifications

B2

How do you categorize the similarities and differences of the message in each article?

Details

B1

Paraphrase the main idea of each article.

George Boole and the Wonderful World of 0s and 1s

by Ems Lord

2015 is a special anniversary for mathematicians. It is the bicentenary of the birth of George Boole, one of the founding fathers of our modern computers. The story of George Boole (1815–1864) is an extraordinary example of collaboration across the centuries. Boole's work provided the foundations for today's computers and mobile phones, yet he died many years before the first computers were invented. How did a mathematician who lived, and died, in the nineteenth century have such an impact on our twenty-first century technology? This the tale of self-taught mathematician George Boole and the modern day engineers who recognised the power of his ideas.

Boole's Early Life

George Boole's early life did not mark him out as a ground-breaking mathematician. Born in Lincoln in 1815, he was the son of a local cobbler and would have been expected to work in the family shoe making business as he grew older. But his father's business collapsed and Boole became a local school teacher instead. By the age of 19, he was already a head teacher, spending his evenings and weekends exploring his mathematical ideas. His initial writings appeared in the Cambridge Mathematics Journal and his work soon attracted the attention of the Royal Society. In 1844 Boole was awarded the Royal Society's Royal Medal for his paper "On a general method of analysis."

His increased profile led to the offer of a professorship in mathematics. Boole left behind his Lincolnshire teaching career and headed off to Cork University to pursue his mathematics full-time, and make the breakthrough that still impacts our lives today.

The Breakthrough

During his time in Ireland, Boole focused on combining logical deduction with algebra. He argued that the logical approach taken by the ancient Greek philosopher Aristotle and his followers was insufficient for addressing certain types of problems. He focused on those problems where individual statements, or propositions, could either be described as true or false. Boole's work required the development of a new branch of algebra and its associated arithmetical rules.

To introduce Boole's ideas, consider these two propositions:

A = David Beckham is a footballer

B = Quidditch is an Olympic sport

We know that one of them is true and the other is false (I'll let you decide which is which!). But what about the statement A AND B: David Beckham is a footballer AND Quidditch is an Olympic sport? It's clearly false! For it to be true, we would need each of A and B to be true, which isn't the case. Therefore, the statement A AND B is false. If we assign the truth value 0 to a false statement and the value 1 to a true one, then we can write the AND connective as a kind of multiplication: AB stands for A AND B, and since one is true and the other false, we see that AB has the truth value $0 \times 1 = 0$.

What about the statement A OR B? David Beckham is a footballer OR Quidditch is an Olympic sport? For this to be true only one of A or B needs to be true, which is the case in our example. Hence A OR B has a truth value of 1. We can write it as a kind of addition: A + B stands for A OR B, and since one is true and the other false, we see that A + B has the truth value $0 + 1 = 1$. These ideas also make sense if A and B swap their truth values, or if they are both true or both false. The tables below show the truth values for A AND B and A OR B for all possible truth value combinations. They also show the corresponding arithmetic operations, as defined by Boole. The only thing that makes Boole's arithmetic different from the arithmetic we are used to is that, for Boole, $1 + 1 = 1$, rather than $1 + 1 = 2$. But that's not too difficult a feature to get used to.

A	B	A and B	A × B
1	1	1	$1 \times 1 = 1$
1	0	0	$1 \times 0 = 0$
0	1	0	$0 \times 1 = 0$
0	0	0	$0 \times 0 = 0$

A	B	A or B	A + B
1	1	1	$1 + 1 = 1$
1	0	1	$1 + 0 = 1$
0	1	1	$0 + 1 = 1$
0	0	0	$0 + 0 = 0$

In the world of Boolean logic all statements are made up of smaller statements connected by AND and OR, and possibly also involving the NOT operation, which turns the truth value of a statement into its opposite: if the statement "David Beckham is a footballer" is true then the statement "David Beckham is NOT a footballer" is false.

Now that you know some of Boole's algebraic laws, you might like the following problem:

Imagine that I have three counters X, Y and Z. They are coloured red, white and blue, but not necessarily in this order. One, but only one, of the following statements is true:

    X is red
    Y is not red
    Z is not blue
    Can you work out the colours of the counters?

Although the problem could be solved in a number of different ways, such as using trial and improvement, Boole argued that his algebra provided a much more systematic approach to problem solving. For the above problem, you may have already noticed several key propositions that will help to solve the problem. For example, we know that X must be either red, white or blue. So, the proposition "X is red, white or blue" is true with the truth value 1. Likewise, the proposition "X or Y or Z is red" must also be true with the truth value 1. We also know that each colour is only used once so the proposition "X and Y are red" is false with truth value 0. Likewise, a counter can only be one colour so the proposition "X is red and blue" is also false with truth value 0.

Working in this way, I will leave you to complete the set of propositions and to use Boole's approach to solve the problem for yourself.

Collaborating Across the Centuries

Boole's binary approach found a powerful application over 70 years after his death, when the mathematician and engineer Claude Shannon realised that it provided the perfect description for electrical circuits. To see how, imagine an electrical circuit with two switches and a light bulb attached to it. The bulb comes on when a current flows through the circuit, otherwise the bulb is off. Each switch can be either on (closed) or off (open). In the left-hand figure below, the light will only come on if both of the switches are on. In the right-hand figure, the light will come on as long as one of the switches is on.

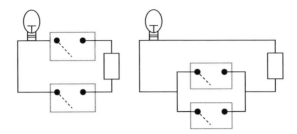

Engineers including Shannon realised that they could write 1 for the "on" position of the bulb and the switches and 0 for the "off" position. Writing down the possible combinations of 0 and 1 for the switches and the corresponding state of the bulb, what you get are exactly the truth tables of AND (left-hand circuit) and OR (right-hand circuit).

Left-hand circuit			Right-hand circuit		
Switch 1	Switch 2	Bulb	Switch 1	Switch 2	Bulb
1	1	1	1	1	1
1	0	0	1	0	1
0	1	0	0	1	1
0	0	0	0	0	0

Using an inverter switch, which allows a current to flow when the switch is open, you can also mimic the truth table of NOT. This realisation meant that engineers could employ Boole's algebraic approach to design and to simplify their circuits. Bur Shannon went further still: he suggested that all types of information—from words to pictures—could be described using strings of 0s and 1s. (In fact, it was Shannon who popularised the term *bit* we use to describe these digits today.) Since you can represent the logical AND, OR and NOT operations using electronic circuits, you can perform all sorts of logical tasks involving this information. It's this fact that the central processing units (CPUs) in our modern day computers are based on.

Whatever electronic gadget you use, it is based on the binary system and algebraic approach to logic first proposed by George Boole. A man who lived and died several years before the first light bulbs came on the market played a pivotal role in the development of the circuitry of our modern world.

Note. From "George Boole and the wonderful world of 0s and 1s" by E. Lord, 2015, *PLUS Magazine*, retrieved from https://plus.maths.org/content/george-boole. Copyright 2015 by E. Lord and NRICH (http://www.nrich.maths.org). Reprinted with permission.

Consequences and Implications

A3

What have been the implications of Boole's discovery, even today?

Cause and Effect

A2

According to the article, what was the effect on fields other than math of having a binary system of operation?

Sequencing

A1

What is the sequence of events that led Boole to learn of the importance of his discovery? What qualities of mind did he have that helped him? How do you know?

GEORGE BOOLE AND THE WONDERFUL WORLD OF 0S AND 1S

Generalizations

B3

Write two specific generalizations you can make about the importance of scientific or mathematical discovery on the future.

Classifications

B2

Classify other types of problems that Boole's system may solve. Why might his system solve these problems? What other examples of Boolean logic applications besides what was listed in the text can you find? Share those with a partner.

Details

B1

Cite examples of how Boole's system works. Try to solve the problem presented in the article and show your thinking.

Focus on the Global Economy

In November 2011, Bill Gates presented a report to the G20, or the Group of 20, an international forum that meets annually to strengthen the global economy and improve global regulations. Gates's report urged G20 leaders to continue to meet their contributions to foreign aid, even if those contributions were burdensome to government budgets.

After the economic collapse in 2008, the G20 met more frequently to solve the global crisis. The G20 supported jobs and open trade, helping to curb some of the economic damage. Still, by 2011, more work was needed to improve the global economy, especially the economies of developing nations.

Gates began his report by praising the efforts of the G20 countries so far. The world economy in 2011 had grown by 500% since 1960. Many countries had increased their GDP, or gross domestic product, the value of goods and services produced in a country. Improvements in agriculture and health had brought the death rate down by 80%, and global poverty rates had decreased as well.

However, Gates noted, countries should not neglect foreign aid at this critical time. According to Gates, innovation is the driving force that will raise countries out of poverty and contribute to the overall success of the global economy. Examples of this innovation include improved medicine and farming. If struggling countries can inoculate more of their citizens against harmful diseases, then those citizens will have a chance to contribute to the economy. Similarly, if new kinds of seeds are developed, then more people will be able to get the nutrition they need. But this innovation cannot happen if poorer countries do not receive aid.

Even wealthy countries could benefit from increased aid to developing nations, Gates argued. He pointed to the explosive growth of Mexico, Indonesia, China, and Brazil in the past few decades. If those countries could partner with less-developed countries, they could share their knowledge and help spur overall growth and improvement.

To help donors reach their aid goals, Gates proposed a few different kinds of taxes. A heavy tobacco tax, for example, would improve overall health while raising revenue. If used, it could generate $170 billion a year, which could then be used to help the development of struggling countries. Gates also proposed a financial transaction tax and a tax on shipping and aviation fuels.

Although these taxes would definitely raise money, some countries, including Canada and the United States, felt the new measures would put too much burden on banks. Business groups warned that the taxes could affect economies negatively by stifling growth. However, Gates urged leaders to remember that foreign aid makes up only 1% of public spending. We can still support developing economies, he said, without feeling the loss in our own countries.

Gates also urged leaders to consider the long-term consequences that decreased aid might bring. Even if cutting aid budgets helped wealthy countries in the short term, it could negatively affect them later. Here Gates brought up environmental concerns. Climate change and economic development are related, he said. If we want farmers to thrive, we need to help them adapt to changing climate conditions. We need to think in the long term—what will the global economy look like in 2050? The Gates report insisted that foreign aid could make all the difference.

References

Gates Foundation. (2011). *Executive summary: A report by Bill Gates to G20 leaders.* Retrieved from http://www.gatesfoundation.org/What-We-Do/Global-Policy/G20-Report

Reuters. (2011). *Bill Gates to G20: Financial transaction tax could raise aid for poorer nations.* Retrieved from http://www.huffingtonpost.com/2011/09/23/bill-gates-g20-taxes-for-poor-nations_n_978395.html

Whittington, L. (2011). Don't strangle foreign aid, Gates to tell G20. *Toronto Star.* Retrieved from http://www.thestar.com/news/canada/2011/11/02/dont_strangle_foreign_aid_gates_to_tell_g20.html

Consequences and Implications

A3

What are the implications of having a master plan to relieve poverty throughout the world? What are the implications of not having one?

Cause and Effect

A2

Who is the audience for the paper? In what way is that audience appealed to? What effect would the paper have on them?

Sequencing

A1

Analyze the sequencing of ideas of the Gates article. How effectively is it organized? Explain your thinking.

Creative Synthesis

D3

Create a secondary proposal to Gates, highlighting one of the ideas for helping and arguing why it is the most important to implement.

Summarizing

D2

What are the ideas presented for solutions to the problems of poverty around the world? How effective might each one be, based on your understanding of the issue?

Paraphrasing

D1

What data and evidence does Gates present to support the need for support around the world? How credible did you find the argument? Explain your thinking.

FOCUS ON THE GLOBAL ECONOMY

Social Studies

Section 3 includes the selected readings and accompanying question sets for each social studies selection. Each reading is followed by up to three sets of questions; each set is aligned to one of the six ladder skills.

The ladder skills covered by each selection are as follows:

Reading Titles	Ladders	Comparison Ladder
Excerpt From "Seeing Red: The Cold War and American Public Opinion"	B, D	
Excerpt From "Their Finest Hour"	A, B, D	
Woman's Rights to the Suffrage	A, D	D
Ain't I a Woman?	B, E	D

Excerpt From "Seeing Red: The Cold War and American Public Opinion"

by John Kenneth White, Department of Politics, Catholic University of America

The Structure of American Public Opinion During the Cold War

In 1949, Arthur M. Schlesinger, Jr., wrote of the Cold War: "In its essence this crisis is internal." Although Schlesinger believed that the external communist threat was real, he believed that its real danger was the fear it engendered in the minds of most Americans. Schlesinger proved prescient, as the resultant politics of fear prompted many to contrast their own ideological thinking with communism. As Richard Nixon once observed, "People respond more to fear than love. They don't teach you that in Sunday school, but it's true."

Fear is a powerful political weapon, especially in such a highly ideological nation as the United States. Political scientist Louis Hartz once hypothesized that Americans were so ideologically straight-jacketed that a philosophy that did not espouse individualism, equality of opportunity, and freedom would be seen as alien. Alexis de Tocqueville held a similar view, writing in *Democracy in America* (1835): "I know of no country in which there is so little independence of mind and real freedom of discussion as in America." . . .

As the decades passed and with no end of the Cold War in sight, communism became the antithesis to the American creed. In 1964, the World Book Encyclopedia drew a bright line between communism and American-style democracy:

> In a democratic country, the government rules by consent of the people. In a communist country, the dictator rules by force and stays in power by force. A democratic government tries to act in a way that will benefit the people. . . . Under communism, the interests of the gov-

ernment always come first. . . . Communism violently opposes democracy and the democratic way of life.

These views were shared by the vast majority of Americans.

Note. Excerpted from "Seeing Red: The Cold War and American Public Opinion" by J. K. White, n.d., retrieved from http://www.archives.gov/research/foreign-policy/cold-war/conference/white.html

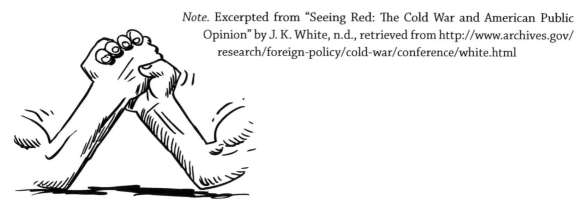

EXCERPT FROM "SEEING RED: THE COLD WAR AND AMERICAN PUBLIC OPINION"

Generalizations

B3

What generalizations might you make about fear and public opinion from reading this excerpt?

Classifications

B2

Categorize how the American public opinion was "structured" during the Cold War, based on the excerpt.

Details

B1

What details might you cite from the piece to support the concept of fear? How is the concept of fear explained in the piece? To what effect?

Creative Synthesis

D3

Have a quick debate with your classmates (stand on opposite sides of the room based on your opinion) explaining whether or not fear is a more powerful motivator than love. Use evidence from this speech as well as at least two different current events to support your answer.

Summarizing

D2

Summarize the argument White is trying to make about the structuring of public opinion versus free thinking.

Paraphrasing

D1

Paraphrase what Alexis de Tocqueville meant when he wrote: "I know of no country in which there is so little independence of mind and real freedom of discussion as in America." Why did White use this quote? How did it help him with his argument?

EXCERPT FROM "SEEING RED: THE COLD WAR AND AMERICAN PUBLIC OPINION"

Excerpt From "Their Finest Hour"

*Winston Churchill, June 18, 1940, Speech
to the House of Commons*

. . . I have thought it right upon this occasion to give the House and the country some indication of the solid, practical grounds upon which we base our inflexible resolve to continue the war. There are a good many people who say, "Never mind. Win or lose, sink or swim, better die than submit to tyranny—and such a tyranny." And I do not dissociate myself from them. But I can assure them that our professional advisers of the three Services unitedly advise that we should carry on the war, and that there are good and reasonable hopes of final victory. We have fully informed and consulted all the self-governing Dominions, these great communities far beyond the oceans who have been built up on our laws and on our civilization, and who are absolutely free to choose their course, but are absolutely devoted to the ancient Motherland, and who feel themselves inspired by the same emotions which lead me to stake our all upon duty and honor. We have fully consulted them, and I have received from their Prime Ministers, Mr. Mackenzie King of Canada, Mr. Menzies of Australia, Mr. Fraser of New Zealand, and General Smuts of South Africa—that wonderful man, with his immense profound mind, and his eye watching from a distance the whole panorama of European affairs—I have received from all these eminent men, who all have Governments behind them elected on wide franchises, who are all there because they represent the will of their people, messages couched in the most moving terms in which they endorse our decision to fight on, and declare themselves ready to share our fortunes and to persevere to the end. That is what we are going to do.

We may now ask ourselves: In what way has our position worsened since the beginning of the war? It has worsened by the fact that the Germans have conquered a large part of the coast line of Western Europe, and many small countries have been overrun by them. This aggravates the possibilities of air attack and adds to our naval preoccupations. It in no way diminishes, but on the contrary definitely increases, the power of our long-distance blockade. Similarly, the entrance of Italy into the war increases the power of our long-distance blockade. We have stopped the worst leak by that. We do not know whether military resistance will come to an end in France or not, but should it do so, then of course the Germans will be able to concentrate their forces, both military and industrial, upon us. But for the reasons I have given to the House these will not be found so easy to apply. If invasion has become more imminent, as no doubt it has, we, being relieved from the task of maintaining a large army in France, have far larger and more efficient forces to meet it.

If Hitler can bring under his despotic control the industries of the countries he has conquered, this will add greatly to his already vast armament output. On the other hand, this will not happen immediately, and we are now assured of immense, continuous and increasing support in supplies and munitions of all kinds from the United States; and especially of aeroplanes and pilots from the Dominions and across the oceans coming from regions which are beyond the reach of enemy bombers.

I do not see how any of these factors can operate to our detriment on balance before the winter comes; and the winter will impose a strain upon the Nazi regime, with almost all Europe writhing and starving under its cruel heel, which, for all their ruthlessness, will run them very hard. We must not forget that from the moment when we declared war on the 3rd September it was always possible for Germany to turn all her Air Force upon this country, together with any other devices of invasion she might conceive, and that France could have done little or nothing to prevent her doing so. We have, therefore, lived under this danger, in principle and in a slightly modified form, during all these months. In the meanwhile, however, we have enormously improved our methods of defense, and we have learned what we had no right to assume at the beginning, namely, that the individual aircraft and the individual British pilot have a sure and definite superiority. Therefore, in casting up this dread balance sheet and contemplating our dangers with a disillusioned eye, I see great reason for intense vigilance and exertion, but none whatever for panic or despair.

During the first four years of the last war the Allies experienced nothing but disaster and disappointment. That was our constant fear: one blow after another, terrible losses, frightful dangers. Everything miscarried. And yet at the end of those four years the morale of the Allies was higher than that of the Germans, who had moved from one aggressive triumph to another, and who stood everywhere triumphant invaders of the lands into which they had broken. During that war we repeatedly asked ourselves the question: How are we going to win? and no one was able ever to answer it with much precision, until at the end, quite suddenly, quite unexpectedly, our terrible foe collapsed before us, and we were so glutted with victory that in our folly we threw it away.

We do not yet know what will happen in France or whether the French resistance will be prolonged, both in France and in the French Empire overseas. The French Government will be throwing away great opportunities and casting adrift their future if they do not continue the war in accordance with their Treaty obligations, from which we have not felt able to release them. The House will have read the historic declaration in which, at the desire of many Frenchmen—and of our own hearts—we have proclaimed our willingness at the darkest hour in French history to conclude a union of common citizenship in this struggle. However matters may go in France or with the French Government, or other French Governments, we in this Island and in the British Empire will never lose our sense of comradeship with the French people. If we are now called upon to endure what they have been suffering, we shall emulate their courage, and if final victory rewards our toils they shall share the gains, aye, and freedom shall be restored to all. We abate nothing of our just demands; not one jot or tittle do we recede. Czechs, Poles, Norwegians, Dutch, Belgians have joined their causes to our own. All these shall be restored.

What General Weygand called the Battle of France is over. I expect that the Battle of Britain is about to begin. Upon this battle depends the survival of Christian civilization. Upon it depends our own British life, and the long continuity of our institutions and our Empire. The whole fury and might of the enemy must very soon be turned on us. Hitler knows that he will have to break us in this Island or lose the war. If we can stand up to him, all Europe may be free and the life of the world may move forward into broad, sunlit uplands. But if we fail, then the whole world, including the United States, including all that we have known and cared for, will sink into the abyss of a new Dark Age made more sinister, and perhaps more protracted, by the lights of perverted science. Let us therefore brace ourselves to our duties, and so bear ourselves that, if the British Empire and its Commonwealth last for a thousand years, men will still say, "This was their finest hour."

Note. Excerpted from "Their Finest Hour," by W. Churchill, 1940, retrieved from http://www.winstonchurchill.org/resources/speeches/233-1940-the-finest-hour/122-their-finest-hour

Consequences and Implications

A3

What might the consequences have been for Britain if the U.S. had not provided assistance during World War II? How do you know?

Cause and Effect

A2

What does Churchill infer was the cause of the war? What effect has it had at the point of his speech?

Sequencing

A1

What was the sequence of events that Churchill is recounting regarding World War II in the speech? What has preceded the Battle of Britain and why does Churchill believe this is important?

EXCERPT FROM "THEIR FINEST HOUR"

Generalizations

B3

What generalizations might be made about the intent of Churchill's speech? Write a three-paragraph speech that has the same intent as Churchill's regarding another major world conflict.

Classifications

B2

How would you categorize the reasons that Churchill provides for thinking England may win the war?

Details

B1

Provide details from the speech that support the idea that Churchill plans to support the war against Germany at all costs.

EXCERPT FROM "THEIR FINEST HOUR"

Name: _____ Date: _____

Creative Synthesis

D3

Create an artistic portrait of Churchill that conveys his leadership qualities at the moment of this famous speech. It may be a poem, a graphic organizer, a symbol, or a drawing.

Summarizing

D2

Provide a summary of the speech in 150 words. What are the most important ideas shared?

Paraphrasing

D1

Paraphrase the last paragraph of the speech in your own words. Churchill chose his words carefully to evoke emotion. What are some examples of his phrases or words that do so?

EXCERPT FROM "THEIR FINEST HOUR"

Woman's Rights to the Suffrage

Susan B. Anthony, 1873

Friends and Fellow Citizens: I stand before you tonight under indictment for the alleged crime of having voted at the last presidential election, without having a lawful right to vote. It shall be my work this evening to prove to you that in thus voting, I not only committed no crime, but, instead, simply exercised my citizen's rights, guaranteed to me and all United States citizens by the National Constitution, beyond the power of any State to deny.

The preamble of the Federal Constitution says:

"We, the people of the United States, in order to form a more perfect union, establish justice, insure domestic tranquility, provide for the common defense, promote the general welfare, and secure the blessings of liberty to ourselves and our posterity, do ordain and establish this Constitution for the United States of America."

It was we, the people; not we, the white male citizens; nor yet we, the male citizens; but we, the whole people, who formed the Union. And we formed it, not to give the blessings of liberty, but to secure them; not to the half of ourselves and the half of our posterity, but to the whole people—women as well as men. And it is a downright mockery to talk to women of their enjoyment of the blessings of liberty while they are denied the use of the only means of securing them provided by this democratic-republican government—the ballot.

For any State to make sex a qualification that must ever result in the disfranchisement of one entire half of the people is to pass a bill of attainder, or an ex post facto law, and is therefore a violation of the supreme law of the land. By it the blessings of liberty are forever withheld from women and their female posterity. To them this government has no just powers derived from the consent of the governed. To them this government is not a democracy. It is not a republic. It is an odious aristocracy; a hateful oligarchy of sex; the most hateful aristocracy ever established on the face of the globe; an oligarchy of wealth, where the right govern the poor. An oligarchy of learning, where the educated govern the ignorant, or even an oligarchy of race, where the Saxon rules the African, might be endured; but this oligarchy of sex, which makes father, brothers, husband, sons, the oligarchs over the mother and sisters, the wife and daughters of every household—which ordains all men sovereigns, all women subjects, carries dissension, discord and rebellion into every home of the nation.

Webster, Worcester and Bouvier all define a citizen to be a person in the United States, entitled to vote and hold office.

The only question left to be settled now is: Are women persons? And I hardly believe any of our opponents will have the hardihood to say they are not. Being persons, then, women are citizens; and no State has a right to make any law, or to enforce any old law, that shall abridge their privileges or immunities. Hence, every discrimination against women in the constitutions and laws of the several States is today null and void, precisely as in every one against Negroes.

Note. From "Woman's Rights to the Suffrage," by S. B. Anthony, 1873, retrieved from http://www.nationalcenter.org/AnthonySuffrage.html. Reprinted from the public domain.

Consequences and Implications

A3

What consequences does Anthony expect as a result of her speech? How do you know? Would an emotional appeal have been a better tactic? Why or why not? (Consider the context of the era as well her purpose.)

Cause and Effect

A2

What is the cause for Anthony's speech? What effect does it have on her own freedom? The reader?

Sequencing

A1

How does Anthony use logical appeals to make her point? Sequence her appeals in order of importance.

WOMAN'S RIGHTS TO THE SUFFRAGE

Creative Synthesis

D3

Create an editorial cartoon or slogan that generalizes Anthony's appeal to her audience.

Summarizing

D2

Summarize the central points of her argument in 100 words or make a bullet outline of her key points.

Paraphrasing

D1

Paraphrase in your own words the argument that Anthony uses to justify her act of voting. Provide at least three aspects of the argument she presents.

WOMAN'S RIGHTS TO THE SUFFRAGE

Ain't I A Woman?

Sojourner Truth, 1851 Women's Convention, Akron, OH

Well, children, where there is so much racket there must be something out of kilter. I think that 'twixt the negroes of the South and the women at the North, all talking about rights, the white men will be in a fix pretty soon. But what's all this here talking about?

That man over there says that women need to be helped into carriages, and lifted over ditches, and to have the best place everywhere. Nobody ever helps me into carriages, or over mud-puddles, or gives me any best place! And ain't I a woman? Look at me! Look at my arm! I have ploughed and planted, and gathered into barns, and no man could head me! And ain't I a woman? I could work as much and eat as much as a man—when I could get it—and bear the lash as well! And ain't I a woman? I have borne thirteen children, and seen most all sold off to slavery, and when I cried out with my mother's grief, none but Jesus heard me! And ain't I a woman?

Then they talk about this thing in the head; what's this they call it? (Member of audience whispers, "intellect") That's it, honey. What's that got to do with women's rights or negroes' rights? If my cup won't hold but a pint, and yours holds a quart, wouldn't you be mean not to let me have my little half measure full?

Then that little man in black there, he says women can't have as much rights as men, 'cause Christ wasn't a woman! Where did your Christ come from? Where did your Christ come from? From God and a woman! Man had nothing to do with Him.

If the first woman God ever made was strong enough to turn the world upside down all alone, these women together ought to be able to turn it back, and get it right side up again! And now they is asking to do it, the men better let them.

Obliged to you for hearing me, and now old Sojourner ain't got nothing more to say.

Note. From "Ain't I a Woman?," by S. Truth, 1851, retrieved from https://legacy.fordham.edu/halsall/mod/sojtruth-woman.asp. Reprinted from the public domain.

Generalizations

B3

What generalizations might you make about equity,
based on the treatment of both women and Black people
at this time in our history? Write at least two.

	Equity Generalizations
Treatment of Women	
Treatment of Black People	

Classifications

B2

How would you classify the ideas she speaks of in her speech?
Make two columns, one labeled Treatment of Women and
one labeled Treatment of Black People for your classification.
How are the examples in each column similar? Different?

Details

B1

What examples of women's ill treatment are evident in the Sojourner
Truth speech? What aspects of the ill treatment of Black people?

Using Emotion

E3

Analyze Truth's argument and her use of logic and emotion to draw in the reader. Which argument appeals most to you and why?

Expressing Emotion

E2

Does Sojourner Truth use more emotion or logic to convey her message? Highlight each type of argument in a different color as you read through the speech a second time. Why do you think she used more of one than the other?

Understanding Emotion

E1

What feelings do you have as you read this text? How does Truth's use of language impact your feelings?

AIN'T I A WOMAN?

Comparison Ladder for "Woman's Rights to the Suffrage" and "Ain't I a Woman?"

Now that your students have read two powerful speeches by the two most prominent women of their time on the issues of women's and Black rights, guide them in discussing the following questions as a way to compare the two speeches and their relative significance in the causes the two women support.

Creative Synthesis

D3

Create a speech that is no more than 2 minutes in length and is modeled on one of the two speech examples, arguing for a cause about which you care. Make the case that legislators need to create a law to enact your ideas. Think about your audience and determine whether you need more logical or emotional appeals.

Summarizing

D2

Which speech is more effective in respect to its impact on the listener? Which speech is more effective in its argument? Explain your thinking, using evidence and techniques discussed in previous ladders.

Paraphrasing

D1

Paraphrase the messages between the two speeches.
How are these alike and different?

The Arts

Section 4 includes selected readings and accompanying question sets in the arts. Each reading is followed by one or two sets of questions; each set is aligned to one of the six ladder skills.

The ladder skills covered by each selection are as follows:

Reading Titles	Ladders	Comparison Ladder
Excerpt From William Faulkner Nobel Prize Banquet Speech, 1950	A, C	C, D
Excerpt From Mario Vargas Llosa Nobel Prize Banquet Speech, 2010	A, C	C, D
Remains of the Past: Roman Art and Architecture	A, B	
Jacob Lawrence	B, C	
Duke Ellington	A, D	

Excerpt From William Faulkner Nobel Prize Banquet Speech, 1950

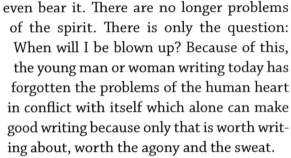

. . . Our tragedy today is a general and universal physical fear so long sustained by now that we can even bear it. There are no longer problems of the spirit. There is only the question: When will I be blown up? Because of this, the young man or woman writing today has forgotten the problems of the human heart in conflict with itself which alone can make good writing because only that is worth writing about, worth the agony and the sweat.

He must learn them again. He must teach himself that the basest of all things is to be afraid; and, teaching himself that, forget it forever, leaving no room in his workshop for anything but the old verities and truths of the heart, the old universal truths lacking which any story is ephemeral and doomed—love and honor and pity and pride and compassion and sacrifice. Until he does so, he labors under a curse. He writes not of love but of lust, of defeats in which nobody loses anything of value, of victories without hope and, worst of all, without pity or compassion. His griefs grieve on no universal bones, leaving no scars. He writes not of the heart but of the glands.

. . . I decline to accept the end of man. It is easy enough to say that man is immortal simply because he will endure: that when the last ding-dong of doom has clanged and faded from the last worthless rock hanging tideless in the last red and dying evening, that even then there will still be one more sound: that of his puny inexhaustible voice, still talking. . . . I believe that man will not merely endure: he will prevail. He is immortal, not because he alone among creatures has an inexhaustible voice, but because he has a soul, a spirit capable of compassion and sacrifice and endurance.

The poet's, the writer's, duty is to write about these things. It is his privilege to help man endure by lifting his heart, by reminding him of the courage and honor and hope and pride and compassion and pity and sacrifice which have been the glory of his past. The poet's voice need not merely be the record of man, it can be one of the props, the pillars to help him endure and prevail.

Note. Excerpted from "Banquet Speech," by W. Faulkner, 1950, retrieved from http://www. nobelprize.org/nobel_prizes/literature/laureates/1949/faulkner-speech.html

Consequences and Implications

A3

What would be Faulkner's idea of the consequences if writers stopped writing about human truth?

Cause and Effect

A2

What are the causes and the effects of having a voice, in his perspective?

Sequencing

A1

What details does Faulkner provide about the value of writers/poets within our society?

EXCERPT FROM WILLIAM FAULKNER NOBEL PRIZE BANQUET SPEECH, 1950

Theme/Concept

C3

What is the theme of his speech? Capture the theme in one sentence or phrase.

Inference

C2

What inferences does he make about the impact of fear?

Textual Elements and Understanding

C1

What elements does Faulkner use to draw you into his speech? Why are these important features for the audience?

EXCERPT FROM WILLIAM FAULKNER NOBEL PRIZE BANQUET SPEECH, 1950

Excerpt From Mario Vargas Llosa Nobel Prize Banquet Speech, 2010

. . . Once upon a time, there was a boy who learned to read at the age of five. This changed his life. Owing to the adventure tales he read, he discovered a way to escape from the poor house, the poor country and the poor reality in which he lived, and to journey to wonderful, mesmerizing places peopled with the most beautiful beings and the most surprising things, where every day and every night brought a more intense, more thrilling more unusual form of bliss.

He so enjoyed reading stories that one day this boy, who was now a young man, took to making them up himself and writing them. He had a hard time doing it, but it brought him pleasure and he delighted in writing tales as much as he delighted in reading them.

The character in my story, however, was very aware that the real world was one thing and the fancy world of dreams and literature quite another, and that the latter only came to light when he read and wrote stories. The rest of the time, it vanished.

Until one day, in the wee hours of the morning, the protagonist of my story received a mysterious call in which a gentleman with a name that defied all pronunciation announced to him that he had won a prize and that in order to receive it he would have to travel to a place called Stockholm, the capital of a land called Sweden (or something of the sort).

To his total bewilderment, my character then started to experience in real life one of those stories that until then he had only found in the unreal and ideal realm of literature. He suddenly felt like the pauper must have felt when he was confused with the prince in Mark Twain's *The Prince and the Pauper*. He is still there, quite startled, not knowing whether he is dreaming or fully awake, whether what is happening is for real or a lie, whether what is occurring is life or literature, because the border that separates the two seems to have totally vanished. . . .

Note. Excerpted from "Banquet Speech," by M. V. Llosa, 2010, retrieved from http://www.nobelprize.org/nobel_prizes/literature/laureates/2010/vargas_llosa-speech_en.html

Consequences and Implications

A3

What are the implications for future writers in the story he told?

Cause and Effect

A2

What effect does the story have on you? How does Llosa create the context for that to happen?

Sequencing

A1

What details does Llosa provide about the boy in the story?

EXCERPT FROM MARIO VARGAS LLOSA NOBEL PRIZE BANQUET SPEECH, 2010

Name: _____ Date: _____

Theme/Concept

C3

What is the theme of the story that Llosa tells?

Inference

C2

What inferences do you draw about the boy's
life growing up from the speech?

Textual Elements and Understanding

C1

Who is the central character in his story?
Where does it take place? How do you know?

EXCERPT FROM MARIO VARGAS LLOSA NOBEL PRIZE BANQUET SPEECH, 2010

Comparison Ladders for "Excerpt From William Faulkner Nobel Prize Banquet Speech, 1950" and "Excerpt From Mario Vargas Llosa Nobel Prize Banquet Speech, 2010"

Two writers, who both received the Nobel Prize for Literature 60 years apart, gave very different speeches to accept their prize. Students may now analyze how these speeches are similar, yet different, and their overall effect on the reader.

Theme/Concept

C3

How did each speech appeal to your emotions? To your thinking about writing? Explain how the central messages and appeals impact your emotions and your thinking about writing.

Inference

C2

Which speech was more effective in your opinion? Why? Justify your perspective using evidence of appeals from both speeches.

Textual Elements and Understanding

C1

What are some of the similarities between the two speeches? What are major differences? Provide evidence to support your point of view.

COMPARISON LADDERS FOR "EXCERPT FROM WILLIAM FAULKNER NOBEL PRIZE BANQUET SPEECH, 1950" AND "EXCERPT FROM MARIO VARGAS LLOSA NOBEL PRIZE BANQUET SPEECH, 2010"

Creative Synthesis

D3

If you were to receive an award for your writing, what would it be for and what would you say? Craft a 150-word acceptance speech that uses emotional appeal and is grounded in the events of the current era.

Summarizing

D2

Summarize how historical context and culture affect presentation and interpretation, based on the two writings.

Paraphrasing

D1

Explain to what extent your reaction to the speeches is grounded in the difference in the eras in which they were presented (i.e., 1950 vs. 2010)? In differences in the nationality of the writer (i.e., American vs. Peruvian)?

COMPARISON LADDERS FOR "EXCERPT FROM WILLIAM FAULKNER NOBEL PRIZE BANQUET SPEECH, 1950" AND "EXCERPT FROM MARIO VARGAS LLOSA NOBEL PRIZE BANQUET SPEECH, 2010"

Remains of the Past: Roman Art and Architecture
The Greatest Roman Artistic Contribution

Perhaps the Romans' greatest contribution to Western civilization was their use of the arch for engineering purposes. This innovation contributed to another important one—the building of aqueducts (aqua = water, duct = lead) that carried water across obstacles to cities throughout the empire. Seen as a practical engineering invention by a culture more pragmatic than their architectural forebears—the Greeks and the Incans, the arch, in separate blocks of stone, represents the intellectual method of "splitting" nature apart and putting it together in new and more effective combinations.

The Romans constructed the arch in the mathematical form of a semi-circle. This ultimately would be reinvented by later Europeans as an oval, which then became the Gothic arch, seen in many cathedrals around the world. This example illustrates the tradition of cultural borrowing and innovation that connects the Romans back to their predecessors and forward to their artistic descendants.

Although Assyrians created the first aqueduct to transport water to their capital city of Nineveh, Romans created a unique form for water transportation based on their arch to create a more stable structure. One of the best-preserved aqueducts from the Roman period is the Pont du Gard near the French city of Arles. Another example of a fine aqueduct can be found in the gargantuan glory of the Segovian aqueduct in Spain, which spans a half-mile of more than 100 double-tiered arches. Totally intact, one can see the workmanship of the Romans in their desire to provide a pragmatic answer to sustaining the life of those in the provinces, or alternatively, allowing the citizens of Rome to enjoy luxurious fountains and public baths.

Public bathing was big business in ancient Rome, and existed in two forms. Balneae were small-scale bath houses, but thermae were large public complexes, with various rooms and pools, from the apodyterium (changing room) to the palaestra (exercise area) to the tepidarium (warm baths) to the caldarium (hot baths) to the frigidarium (cold baths). The Baths of Caracalla, also located in Rome, represented one such imperial structure, built to accommodate 1600 bathers at a time. This building was one of many built on such a grand scale in ancient Rome.

Eternal Forms

Bronze and marble were the preferred tools of the Romans for their sculpture. Often mimicking the Greek Hellenistic style, they favored the subject matter of the gods and great men. However, the beautiful idealized style eventually evolved into a unique Roman realism in which artists depicted figures as real individuals, warts and all, not as perfect models. This was an important development, as their household gods (i.e., the Lares and Penates) were made in the image of real ancestors of the family and stood as an altar to Roman realism in everyday art. Funerary art in the form of sarcophagi provide evidence of Greek and Etruscan influence on Roman art and further elaborate myth and history. The lid of the sarcophagus often depicted the dead in a reclining pose, reminiscent of Etruscan vessels crafted for the same purpose. Stelae or stone relief sculptures used individual features of the deceased to depict likeness in life.

Some statues of Rome's great leaders retain a realistic air even as they seek to promote the greatness of Rome. Some statues weren't so lifelike, however. The Emperor Augustus preferred idealized forms for propaganda purposes. Whenever possible, artists depicted him in monumental size statuary in a commanding position of power. As popular as Augustus and his brokered Pax Romana was in his own time, his own propaganda pieces survive because of their idealized forms that were easily confused with other imperial statues. One of the most famous surviving bronzes of the emperor Augustus on horseback supposedly remains because he was mistaken for Constantine, who was revered in the next stage of history—so much for realistic depiction!

However, under Augustus, the style of Roman statuary changed. It now took on a larger purpose, one of proclaiming the godlike qualities of Rome's leaders, both former and current. Julius Caesar was also portrayed as a larger-than-life leader. In the posthumous work "the green Caesar," he is depicted as all-knowing and all-seeing in a bust of impressive size to commemorate his power and authority during his lifetime. His adopted heir benefitted from this image, and made sure his image would endure. As seen in the British Museum on the head of Augustus statue, the sheer power and assuredness of the gaze leaves no doubt about the leadership of Augustus over much of the known world. His ability to shape his image in art form and retain that image over time represents one of the great examples of human iconography.

Note. From *Ancient Roots and Ruins* (pp. 69–71) by A. Baska and J. VanTassel-Baska, 2014, Waco, TX: Prufrock Press. Copyright 2014 by Prufrock Press. Reprinted with permission.

Consequences and Implications

A3

How do we make our leaders today icons through art?
Create a collage that demonstrates the implications of that principle
at work. How does this compare with the Roman's interpretations?

Cause and Effect

A2

In the second section of the reading on Eternal Forms,
how did Augustus use art for his own purposes? What
were the effects of that technique on the Romans?

Sequencing

A1

What data in the first section of this reading supports the contention
that the arch was the most important Roman invention?

Generalizations

B3

How is the idea that "form follows function" evident in Roman statuary? Use evidence from both sections to support your answer.

Classifications

B2

What categories of Roman art are explored?

Details

B1

How would you describe, in a few words, the key aspects of Roman art explored in both sections of this reading? Why are these important?

REMAINS OF THE PAST: ROMAN ART AND ARCHITECTURE

Jacob Lawrence

Jacob Lawrence was a celebrated African American painter, whose works portrayed the vibrant and often difficult lives of Black Americans in the 20th century.

Jacob was born in 1917 in Atlantic City, NJ. When he was a child, his parents moved north hoping to find a better life outside of the rural South. His parents separated after the move, and Jacob and his two younger siblings lived in foster homes until their mother could support them in Harlem, NY.

Harlem was one of the top destinations for African Americans at that time. Many were leaving the South and moving to New York, where they could engage in the rich culture and traditions found in Harlem. The move was difficult, however. Many of these migrants, who were accustomed to farm life, now found themselves packed in small apartments in a noisy, fast-paced city. They also struggled with poverty and police brutality.

When Jacob arrived in Harlem at 13, he was overwhelmed by the richness of the city. He was enchanted by the colors and patterns of the neighborhoods—the walls, fire escapes, laundry lines, billboards, and electric signs. In his home, his mother decorated with vibrant, homey colors and patterns that influenced Jacob's creativity. It was not long before he discovered art as a means of expression. Although formal art education was almost impossible for Black students to achieve at the time, Harlem was a unique city. Jacob attended art lessons at an afterschool community workshop, the Utopia House, and later joined the Harlem Art Workshop.

At both centers, he worked with artist Charles Alston and became acquainted with other artists and writers of the Harlem Renaissance. (The Harlem Renaissance was a burst of cultural and artistic energy in 1920s Harlem.) Jacob's arrival just a decade later allowed him to meet such figures as Claude McKay, Augusta Savage, Langston Hughes, and Ralph Ellison. These artists and writers understood Jacob's passion for art and encouraged him to keep pursuing his work.

Jacob communicated the emotional life of his neighborhood through his art. He painted scenes and moments from the urban Harlem community in clear shapes, bright colors, and lively patterns. Jacob felt that in painting portraits of the Harlem community he was also painting his own portrait. He also depicted scenes of various African American historical events, which until then had only been passed down by word of mouth.

His dedication to his craft paid off. In 1938, Jacob had his first solo art exhibition, and just 2 years later received a grant to create a series of paintings depicting the African American migration away from the South. Artist

Gwendolyn Knight helped Jacob with this project by preparing panels and helping to write captions for each scene. The two grew close during this time and married in 1941.

That same year, The Migration Series debuted, and Jacob became the first African American artist to be represented by a major New York gallery. He was only 24. Mainstream artists seemed to find something universal and important in his work. This newfound fame and acceptance among White artists was a struggle for Jacob. He had to learn how to engage with an art culture that did not fully represent African Americans. This tension remained with him in his later artwork, which featured masks and tackled questions of identity.

For a short time, Jacob was drafted into the Coast Guard during World War II. His work as a combat artist influenced him heavily, and he painted a series of war paintings when he returned to the U.S. in 1946. His other works included a series of historical American paintings and a series about African American builders. His later artistic works in the 1950s and 1960s featured more experimental art.

Jacob also worked as an art educator throughout his career. He taught at Black Mountain College in North Carolina. In 1971, he became a professor of painting at the University of Washington at Seattle. He was elected in 1983 to the American Academy of Arts and Letters and received many other honors. He continued painting until his death in 2000. Today Jacob Lawrence is known as a man who helped to communicate both the pride and struggles of Black Americans to a wider audience.

References

The Phillips Collection. (n.d.). *Jacob Lawrence (1917–2000)*. Retrieved from http://www.phillipscollection.org/research/american_art/bios/lawrence-bio.htm

DC Moore Gallery. (n.d.). *Jacob Lawrence*. Retrieved from http://www.dcmooregallery.com/artists/jacob-lawrence

Whitney Museum of American Art. (2002). *Meet Jacob Lawrence*. Retrieved from http://whitney.org/www/jacoblawrence/meet/index.html

Teacher's Note

Ladder B focuses on Lawrence's Migration Series paintings found here or other online sources: http://www.phillipscollection.org/migration_series/flash/experience.html. Ladder C focuses on the written biography that is included in this section.

Generalizations

B3

How does the theme of injustice permeate the work of Lawrence? Select one painting you reviewed and use it to describe how Lawrence portrays that theme. Create an artistic piece on the same theme, using a medium you enjoy working with (e.g., collage, drawing, photography, writing).

Classifications

B2

How does Lawrence portray the people in his Migration Series? If they were characters in a book, how would you describe them?

JACOB LAWRENCE

Details

B1

Conduct a search for Lawrence's Migration Series and review the paintings (also found here: http://www.phillipscollection.org/migration_series/flash/experience.html). What is apparent about the setting for each painting? How would you describe it and what does it represent?

Theme/Concept

C3

Create an artistic timeline, along with symbols for each period, that represents Lawrence's life (select at least four symbols). What symbols have you selected and why? Provide a short statement for each.

Inference

C2

Summarize the key markers of talent development in Lawrence's life. Then review the paintings used for Ladder B. What do you know about Lawrence's life that helps you better understand his paintings?

Textual Elements and Understanding

C1

Read the biography of Lawrence. Paraphrase what is written about Lawrence's early life.

JACOB LAWRENCE

Duke Ellington

Duke Ellington lived for 75 years, being born on April 29, 1899 and dying on May 24, 1974. He revolutionized American music during those years, making jazz a respectable idiom. His work made jazz serious music and allowed him to demonstrate the belief that music affected people deeply. He saw music as "the tonal reflection of beauty."

He was raised in Washington, DC, by parents who were both piano players, filling the home with music. Duke began taking piano lessons at age 7.

Duke attended Garnet Elementary School in Washington, DC, and dropped out of Armstrong Manual Training School (high school) where he was studying commercial art. He turned down a scholarship to The Pratt Institute to pursue his interest in music.

Duke had an early interest and talent for the piano and yet he also enjoyed all forms of music. Not restrictive in his interests, however, he loved baseball and worked selling hot dogs in order to watch the Washington Senators. He had an introverted personality and knew how to divert attention from himself and onto the music. He was always considered suave, charismatic, and dapper, even as a young boy, by women. He managed his bands by the use of humor, charm, and an understanding of individual needs. He rarely conducted using a baton. Most often, he sat at the piano and played during each number.

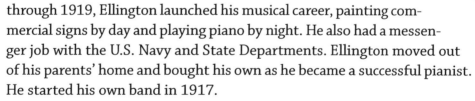

At the age of 14, Ellington created "Soda Fountain Rag" by ear, because he had not yet learned to read and write music. From 1917 through 1919, Ellington launched his musical career, painting commercial signs by day and playing piano by night. He also had a messenger job with the U.S. Navy and State Departments. Ellington moved out of his parents' home and bought his own as he became a successful pianist. He started his own band in 1917.

During the Depression, the recording industry was in crisis, dropping more than 90% of its artists by 1933. Ellington and his orchestra survived the hard times by going on the road in a series of tours. Radio exposure also helped maintain their popularity. He and his band played at the Cotton Club in New York City during the Harlem Renaissance. He lived for music as a mode of life expression during these years and throughout the rest of his life, once saying, "Music is how I live, why I live and how I will be remembered."

Ellington also created music for many of his band members that catered to their individual style, demonstrating his appreciation for individual talents and how they might be expressed and showcased. He became close to Billy Strayhorn, a talented member of the band who also composed and often revised Ellington's work and led the band in his absence. They were highly successful collaborators on many compositions. Ellington did national and international tours with the band, yielding him broader exposure and an international reputation. Duke Ellington led his band from 1923 until his death in 1974, making his work a lifetime endeavor. He also made many recordings of his composed works from the 1930s on and composed scores for films. He actually composed 1000 works for piano and full bands; interestingly, his longer works were less appreciated than his shorter ones.

He married his high school sweetheart. They had one son, Mercer, who also was a musician and business manager for his father's activity. Mercer also took on the responsibility for his father's legacy. His grandson, Paul Ellington, also went into music and created the Duke Ellington Legacy band when his father died.

Ellington received many awards and recognition during his lifetime. He received the Medal of Freedom awarded by President Nixon. He received 12 Grammy Awards from 1959–2000 and was inducted into the Grammy Hall of Fame. Ellington was awarded the Grammy Lifetime Achievement Award in 1966. He received an honorary Ph.D. from Berklee College of Music in 1971. His international reputation was great, as seen in the award of the Legion of Honor from France in 1973. Posthumously, he received the Pulitzer Prize, awarded in 1999. A secondary school was named after him in Washington, DC, providing an educational marker of his influence. His lasting impact has been assured through his songbooks as well as his playing of American jazz. More than any other single person, he was most responsible for the rise of jazz as an American form of music.

References

Biography.com. (n.d.). *Duke Ellington*. Retrieved from http://www.biography.com/people/duke-ellington-9286338

Duke Ellington biography. (2008). Retrieved from http://www.dukeellington.com/ellingtonbio.html

Encyclopaedia Brittanica. (2016). *Duke Ellington: American musician*. Retrieved from http://www.britannica.com/biography/Duke-Ellington

Famous People. (n.d.). *Duke Ellington biography*. Retrieved from http://www.thefamouspeople.com/profiles/duke-ellington-352.php

Wikipedia. (n.d.). *Duke Ellington*. Retrieved from https://en.wikipedia.org/wiki/Duke_Ellington

Consequences and Implications

A3

What were the consequences of Ellington's early development on his later career? Research and trace the development of three other musicians of your choosing and compare their early development to their later development. Is it comparable to Ellington? What can you generalize about the development of musicians, based on your findings?

Cause and Effect

A2

Explain the most significant influences on Duke Ellington's career and the effects these influences had on his success. Use the chart below to help you.

Cause	Example From Life	Effect	Example From Life

Sequencing

A1

How would you sequence the most important events in the life of Duke Ellington? What were the markers as he grew and developed?

Creative Synthesis

D3

Write a note to an aspiring musician that characterizes the most important things they can do to develop their talent based on Duke Ellington's career trajectory as well as your research from Ladder A3 or other musicians you know. Be sure to explain your advice using evidence from the lives of famous musicians including Ellington.

Summarizing

D2

Summarize Ellington's accomplishments as a musician by creating a symbol or metaphor that characterizes his life. Be ready to defend your idea using evidence from the text.

DUKE ELLINGTON

Paraphrasing

D1

If you were asked to create a tweet to paraphrase Duke Ellington's life, what would you tweet? Why?

Part III: Readings and Student Ladder Sets for Fiction and Nonfiction Comparisons

Part III includes the selected readings and accompanying question sets for each nonfiction and fiction comparison selection. Each reading is followed by one or two sets of questions; each set is aligned to one of the six ladder skills.

The ladder skills covered by each selection are as follows:

Reading Titles	Ladders	Comparison Ladder
Break, Break, Break	D, F	E
Korean War Photo Analysis	C	
Composed Upon Westminster Bridge, September 3, 1802	C, F	C
William Wordsworth	A	
At the Window	A	B
D. H. Lawrence	C	
Bond and Free	C, D	C
The Importance of Critical Thinking	A, B, D	
The World Is Too Much With Us	C, F	C
Should Schools Replace Textbooks With Tablets?	B, D	

Break, Break, Break

by Lord Alfred Tennyson

Break, break, break,
On thy cold gray stones, O Sea!
And I would that my tongue could utter
The thoughts that arise in me.

O well for the fisherman's boy,
That he shouts with his sister at play!
O well for the sailor lad,
That he sings in his boat on the bay!

And the stately ships go on
To their haven under the hill:
But O for the touch of a vanish'd hand,
And the sound of a voice that is still!

Break, break, break,
At the foot of thy crags, O Sea!
But the tender grace of a day that is dead
Will never come back to me.

Creative Synthesis

D3

Create or select a symbol that characterizes this poem and the author's message. Use evidence from the poem to justify your symbol selection.

Summarizing

D2

Summarize the message the author wants to convey.
How do you know? Cite evidence from the poem.

Paraphrasing

D1

Tennyson lost a dear childhood friend. Some scholars say that this poem is about the loss of his friend. What do you think? In your own words, describe how this poem is about loss and grief. What other themes do you think it may be conveying?

BREAK, BREAK, BREAK

F3

Playing With Words

Create a poem, using the same rhyme scheme and repetition of words to create mood. Use the 4-stanza model as Tennyson did on a different theme of your choice. Be ready to discuss the theme of your poem and how you used a specific rhyming scheme and repetition of words to create the mood of the poem and to convey meaning.

F2

Thinking About Words

How is repetition and rhyme scheme used to set the mood of the poem and convey its message?

F1

Understanding Words

The rhyme scheme and repetition of words in the poem dictates its sound. Which lines rhyme and which words are used in repetition? Why is this important?

BREAK, BREAK, BREAK

Korean War Photo Analysis

"A grief-stricken American infantryman whose buddy has been killed in action is comforted by another soldier. In the background a corpsman methodically fills out casualty tags, Haktong-ni area, Korea." Photo by Sfc. Al Chang, August 28, 1950, National Archives and Records Administration, Records of the Office of the Chief Signal Officer (111-SC-347803) [VENDOR # 122]. Retrieved from https://catalog.archives.gov/id/531370. Reprinted from the public domain.

Theme/Concept

C3

What message or theme was the photographer trying to convey about the war? How did he achieve his goal?

Inference

C2

Why do you think the photographer chose to include the man filling out the casualty papers in the photo instead of just taking a close-up of the two men or cutting out the man in the background?

Textual Elements and Understanding

C1

What details in this photo and description tell us where the photo was taken? Why is this significant in understanding the purpose?

KOREAN WAR PHOTO ANALYSIS

Comparison Ladder for "Break, Break, Break" and "Korean War Photo Analysis"

The pairing of the photograph from a war zone in the Korean War with a poem from the Victorian Period in England demonstrates how different events can provoke similar responses. Students can now evaluate both forms of media in respect to their effectiveness for the purpose they were developed.

Using Emotion

E3

Create one title for both the poem and the photograph that is appropriate for each and conveys the same overall message. Be ready to justify your title, using evidence from both selections.

Expressing Emotion

E2

How do social media outlets such as Facebook, Instagram, Twitter, or YouTube capture feelings and moments in time? How are these similar to or different from the expressions in more typical media, such as a poem or a photograph? Which do you prefer and why?

Understanding Emotion

E1

Reread the poem and examine the photo. What feelings are evoked in each piece of art? What devices did the poet and photographer use to evoke feelings? Create a Venn diagram to compare their devices.

COMPARISON LADDER FOR "BREAK, BREAK, BREAK" AND "KOREAN WAR PHOTO ANALYSIS"

Composed Upon Westminster Bridge, September 3, 1802
by William Wordsworth

Earth has not any thing to show more fair:
Dull would he be of soul who could pass by
A sight so touching in its majesty:
This City now doth, like a garment, wear
The beauty of the morning; silent, bare,
Ships, towers, domes, theatres, and temples lie
Open unto the fields, and to the sky;
All bright and glittering in the smokeless air.
Never did sun more beautifully steep
In his first splendour, valley, rock, or hill;
Ne'er saw I, never felt, a calm so deep!
The river glideth at his own sweet will:
Dear God! the very houses seem asleep;
And all that mighty heart is lying still!

Name: _____   Date: _____

Theme/Concept

C3

Wordsworth's last line of the poem is: "And all that mighty heart is lying still!" Whose heart is it? Why is it mighty? How does this last line help you understand the meaning of the poem? Is the poem more about how the author feels about his setting or the setting itself?

Inference

C2

What is the setting of this poem, according to the clues the author provides? Quickly sketch the setting described, using clues from the poem to capture the scene. Describe what you have included in the sketch and why.

Textual Elements and Understanding

C1

How does the author feel about his setting in the poem and how do you know?

COMPOSED UPON WESTMINSTER BRIDGE, SEPTEMBER 3, 1802

Playing With Words

F3

Write a poem about the city you know best or your hometown, standing from a high point (such as a bridge) overlooking it at sunset. Use examples of personification, simile, metaphor, and other devices to provide a visual image and create the setting. The chart in F2 can help you.

Thinking About Words

F2

If you were to describe a place that is dear to you, what human attributes might you give it? What would you compare it to and why? Use the following chart to organize your ideas.

The Place	Human Characteristics	Comparisons

Understanding Words

F1

What literary devices does Wordsworth use to make the poem come alive? List examples of personification, simile, metaphor, and other devices.

COMPOSED UPON WESTMINSTER BRIDGE, SEPTEMBER 3, 1802

William Wordsworth

William Wordsworth was one of the defining poets of the Romantic Age in English literature. He championed lyric poetry, the importance of the individual, the integrity of the common man, and humans' relationship to nature.

Born in 1770 in Cumberland, England, William seemed to have an idyllic childhood, which he recounted later in his book-length poem, *The Prelude*. He lived in Cockermouth, a lush rural area near a river, in a large home with a garden. He was close to his siblings, especially his sister Dorothy, who continued to be a source of support and inspiration to him throughout his career. He was taught to read by his mother and encouraged to avail himself of his father's library, which he did as a child growing up. His father worked as a legal representative and was often away from the home on business. Nonetheless, his father urged him to memorize long verses of poetry from the great English poets including Milton and Shakespeare.

Unfortunately, this tranquility dissolved when William's mother, father, and sister Ann died within a few years of each other, and Dorothy was sent away to another household. William attended grade school in the Hawkshead area, and became interested in poetry. He may have even started composing poems at this time, but his actual writing career did not take off until later in his life.

William attended St. John's College in Cambridge, but was not the most dedicated student. In the summer before his final semester, he visited France and encountered the ideas of the French Revolution. There, he gained a greater interest in politics and democracy. He had great sympathy for common people, a theme that appears often in his poems.

His trip to France launched his poetic career, and he published his first collection, *Descriptive Sketches*, in 1793 when he was 23 years old. In 1795, he moved back to England and turned his full energy to poetry. He met Samuel Taylor Coleridge, a fellow poet who greatly influenced him and even proposed poems for William to write. Their friendship and collaboration over the next few years led to the writing of many poems that later comprised the *Lyrical Ballads*. These poems, including the famous "Tintern Abbey," were different from most poetry being released at the time. William used plain language and wrote about everyday people rather than historical figures or gods.

He also wrote a preface to *Lyrical Ballads* that outlines some of his guiding poetic philosophy. Poetry, William believed, should be the "real language of men" and should come from "the spontaneous overflow of feelings . . . recollected in tranquility." In other words, poets should write about real life and real feelings, but wait to do so until they can reflect upon events with wisdom and clarity. He also believed that being outside in nature provided the perfect setting and subject matter for poetry.

From 1798–1808, William wrote many of his most famous poems and became more accepted as a poet. Throughout the years, he also worked on *The Prelude*, a poem that chronicled the development of his spiritual life. This was the first work of its kind—most poets had not believed that one's inner journey was worthy of such attention.

He continued to write poetry during the 1800s, although he slowed his work while he was raising his family. He also lost two of his children to disease, which may have discouraged his interest in writing altogether. He became poet Laureate of England just 7 years before he died. *The Prelude* was published after his death in 1850. Wordsworth inspired legions of poets that followed him with his lyrical language and focus on nature and the common man. Romanticism could not have taken off without his dedication to craft and boundless inspiration. He is buried at Grasmere in the lake region near Dove Cottage, where he and his sister Dorothy had lived for many years.

References

Academy of American Poets. (n.d.). *William Wordsworth*. Retrieved from https://www.poets.org/poetsorg/poet/william-wordsworth

Poetry Foundation. (n.d.). *William Wordsworth (1770–1850)*. Retrieved from http://www.poetryfoundation.org/bio/william-wordsworth

Consequences and Implications

A3

What were the consequences of relationships (or lack thereof) on Wordsworth's life and work? Cite examples from the biography to justify your ideas.

Cause and Effect

A2

If you were to prioritize the most critical events that affected Wordsworth's writing, what would those be and why?

Sequencing

A1

Create a timeline to show the sequence of life events that most affected the work of Wordsworth.

WILLIAM WORDSWORTH

Comparison Ladder for "Composed Upon Westminster Bridge, September 3, 1802" and "William Wordsworth"

The poetry of the Romantic poet Wordsworth has resonated across the years since his death. As students examine major aspects of his life, they can begin to see connections between his poetry and his life.

Theme/Concept

C3

How did the themes mentioned in the biography relate to the poem you read by Wordsworth? How are his life themes and poetry themes similar? What are the differences?

Inference

C2

The biography states that Wordsworth wrote poems that focused on nature and the common man. How does the poem you read support this statement? Why might he choose to write these types of poems based on different life experiences?

Textual Elements and Understanding

C1

How does Wordsworth use personification in the poem? What are examples of it? In what way does the use of that literary device relate to his personal beliefs about the importance of nature as noted in the biography?

COMPARISON LADDER FOR "COMPOSED UPON WESTMINSTER BRIDGE, SEPTEMBER 3, 1802" AND "WILLIAM WORDSWORTH"

At the Window
by D. H. Lawrence

The pine-trees bend to listen to the autumn wind as it mutters
Something which sets the black poplars ashake with hysterical laughter;
While slowly the house of day is closing its eastern shutters.

Further down the valley the clustered tombstones recede,
Winding about their dimness the mist's grey cerements, after
The street lamps in the darkness have suddenly started to bleed.

The leaves fly over the window and utter a word as they pass
To the face that leans from the darkness, intent, with two dark-filled eyes
That watch forever earnestly from behind the window glass.

Consequences and Implications

A3

What are the implications of this scene on the face in the window? If you were that face, create a response to the scene that also uses personification and imagery and responds to the message of the poem.

Cause and Effect

A2

What is the effect of using personification* in this poem on the reader? Where does Lawrence use it and what characteristics does he assign to each object? Make a chart that illustrates this (put the poem's personification in the first column and what is personified in the second column).

*Personification is the assignment of human characteristics to inanimate objects.

Sequencing

A1

What is the sequence of activities in the scene that Lawrence has painted for us?

AT THE WINDOW

D. H. Lawrence

David Herbert Lawrence was an influential English writer who valued immediacy, emotion, and spontaneity in his writing. Though better known as a novelist, he wrote many poems that influenced the course of poetry in the 20th century. He is often referred to as Modernist because he and other Modernist poets ventured from the typical rhyme and verse and used different prose or forms of expression to explain their thoughts.

Lawrence was born in 1885 in Eastwood, Nottinghamshire, England. His father worked as a coal miner, while his mother worked in lace making. His mother's love of literature influenced him greatly in those early years. Lawrence was prone to illness as a child and didn't fit in with many of his peers. Reading and writing became a source of strength and vitality for him.

He wrote his first poems in 1909 when he was 24 years old. These early works featured traditional forms with rigid patterns and rhythms, but as he published more work, he began to experiment with free verse. Composing in free verse allowed him to vary the length of his poetry in an organic and more emotional way. Many of these poems featured animals described in lush detail—almost like people, with complex thoughts and emotions.

Lawrence's reliance on imagery influenced fellow poet Ezra Pound and the Imagist movement. The Imagists captured images in clear, brief poems that relied heavily on the five senses. They were less interested in the lengthy narratives of traditional poetry. Although Lawrence agreed with many of their views, he declined Ezra Pound's invitation to join the movement because he didn't want to be limited to one kind of poetry.

Lawrence was a rebellious and radical writer. He believed that the world had become too industrialized and modern, and he hoped his writing could encourage readers to access their natural instincts. His books were even censored on occasion because readers found them to be too extreme for English society.

His strong opinions earned him many enemies. During World War I, he left England for a voluntary exile—what he called "a savage pilgrimage"—across Europe and into the United States. During this time, he moved from place to place and was ill for much of his travelling. He died of tuberculosis in 1930 at only 44 years old.

Although many of his colleagues dismissed him because of his strong personality, present-day critics consider him a serious writer with artistic integrity. The power of his imagery and emotional content greatly impacted modern poetry and helped shape the course of English literature.

References

Academy of American Poets. (n.d.). *D. H. Lawrence*. Retrieved from https://www.poets.org/poetsorg/poet/d-h-lawrence

Biography.com. (n.d.). *D. H. Lawrence*. Retrieved from http://www.biography.com/people/dh-lawrence-17175776#synopsis

Poetry Foundation. (n.d.). *D. H. Lawrence (1885–1930)*. Retrieved from http://www.poetryfoundation.org/bio/d-h-lawrence

Theme/Concept

C3

If you could describe the theme of Lawrence's life and work in a short phrase, what would the theme be and why?

Inference

C2

Why did Lawrence write? What was his motivation? How do you know?

Textual Elements and Understanding

C1

What were the important aspects and influences of Lawrence's life? In a timeline, list the markers that define who he was from an early age.

D. H. LAWRENCE

Comparison Ladder for "At the Window" and "D. H. Lawrence"

The poetry of D. H. Lawrence and his disdain for the Industrial Revolution were evident in many of his writings. As students examine major aspects of his life, they can begin to see connections between his writing and his life.

B3 — Generalizations

What might you generalize about the face in
the window and the life of Lawrence?

B2 — Classifications

We often see a relationship between life and work. What aspects
of Lawrence's life appeared to influence his work? Use the chart
below to categorize your findings, using the biography and
examples from the poem that illustrate this interaction.

Aspects of Lawrence's Life	Aspects of Lawrence's Poetry	How Do They Interact?

B1 — Details

What are some examples of Lawrence's style, as noted in the
biography? How are these examples related in the poem?

Bond and Free
by Robert Frost

Love has earth to which she clings
With hills and circling arms about—
Wall within wall to shut fear out.
But Thought has need of no such things,
For Thought has a pair of dauntless wings.

On snow and sand and turf, I see
Where Love has left a printed trace
With straining in the world's embrace.
And such is Love and glad to be.
But Thought has shaken his ankles free.

Thought cleaves the interstellar gloom
And sits in Sirius' disc all night,
Till day makes him retrace his flight,
With smell of burning on every plume,
Back past the sun to an earthly room.

His gains in heaven are what they are.
Yet some say Love by being thrall
And simply staying possesses all
In several beauty that Thought fares far
To find fused in another star.

Theme/Concept

C3

Argue in whatever format you choose (essay, poem, graphic) that Love is superior to Thought or that Thought is better than Love. Does Frost suggest that we should choose one state over the other? Explain your thinking.

Inference

C2

How do we know that Frost sees Thought as free? What evidence can you present to support that point of view?

Textual Elements and Understanding

C1

What does the title infer about the poem? Why is it an apt one?

Creative Synthesis

D3

Create a poem that uses two new concepts (like Thought and Love) to show how the concepts are different yet work together. (Example concepts might be: anger, hate, esteem, fear, pain, comfort, peace.) Model your work on the poem just read, creating four stanzas of verse in the same rhyme scheme.

Summarizing

D2

In what ways does Love gain more by staying still versus traveling daily as Thought does? Summarize the argument for staying versus going.

Paraphrasing

D1

What is dangerous about Thought? For example, who is referenced in "the smell of burning on every plume"? About Love? Compare the two images that Frost employs in the poem.

BOND AND FREE

The Importance of Teaching Critical Thinking

Why is critical thinking important to learn and practice in schools? In a technological environment that requires thinking on the part of everyone in the educational sphere, one might argue it is one of the new three C's as opposed to the three R's of reading, writing, and 'rithmetic. The new repetition of letters and words that are the basis for reform curriculum now are: critical thinking, creative thinking (innovation), and communication. Yet critical thinking underlays all of communication and allows creative thinking to take hold at a deeper level. So it is the most important set of skills we might impart to our students.

Standards and Critical Thinking

The new widely adopted education standards, the Common Core State Standards (CCSS) and the Next Generation Science Standards (NGSS), both require a specific set of critical thinking skills in the learning of content. In mathematics, the skill set includes problem solving, based on data and evidence, mathematical reasoning, and inferencing. In language arts, the skills noted are reasoning, evidence, inference, and framing questions. In science, the terminology follows the scientific research model of questions, hypotheses, data or evidence, conclusions (inferences), and implications.

Promoting Depth of Understanding

Even if the new standards and their accompanying assessments did not require critical thinking, they still should prevail as a staple in the curriculum at elementary levels and beyond as they provide the pathway to deep understanding of content. In writing and in speaking, students reveal what they think and how they think about it. In these two acts, teachers have teachable moments when misconceptions can be erased, probing questions asked, and new knowledge gained in each subject area. They also are the most important modes of communicating our thoughts both formally and informally. For example, texting has become a popular mode of communication that requires even tighter use of critical thinking in order to convey purpose.

Critical Thinking as a Bridge Across Disciplines

Thinking skills also raise the level of thought to one that allows inter-disciplinary connections to be made easily. If we can think critically, then we can see connections among different texts, among different images, and across broad-based concepts that bind the disciplines together. I can hold a conversation with a mathematician about a mathematical system and an engineer about a software system while also engaging a physicist in a dialogue about cosmic systems. I can also think about language systems in the same way I think about social science systems, such as families and communities, because the thinking required to do those comparisons is at a high level where I am engaging in deductive reasoning, inferencing, and using data and evidence to understand the connections across these domains of thought.

What Is Critical Thinking in Today's World?

But how do we define critical thinking and what skill set is most important to be taught? We think about higher level thinking as synonymous with analysis, synthesis, and evaluation. Yet we have had another model of critical thinking in our midst for the last 30 years that transforms specific skills into a process of thinking that works in the real world, that helps us see how we reason about the every-day and how we think about world issues that matter and about how the world is organized. The model also defines the habits of mind relevant to critical thought and provides examples of how thinking can be applied to each discipline in a concrete way.

A model of critical thought. In his 1992 book on critical thinking in a changing world, Richard Paul made the point that we live in an ever-changing world. Just as the world has changed, so too has our way of approaching critical thinking education-ally as a system to be understood in all of its elements and interactions. To meet the goal of technological and scientific excellence, we must ensure that students can think critically, creatively, and collaboratively.

Why is teaching critical thinking the most important set of skills? Because it prepares students for life in the 21st century where they must be able to think and reason about new content, new ideas, and grapple with old issues in new contexts. In order to do well in any profession, critical thinking is a prerequisite. Why has research become so popular as an offering to undergraduates at prestigious universities?

Because it helps students internalize a way of thinking about their world that leads to new discoveries and breakthroughs. The process of research itself is critical thinking according to a framework. A model of critical thinking, learned well early, may serve a student for a lifetime.

Conclusion

Thus, whether we teach primary students or university undergraduates, teaching critical thinking is foundational to our work and central to the future of our students. Having a population who can think, read, and write well portends positive outcomes for our society in this century.

Consequences and Implications

A3

What implications do you draw from the essay
on the importance of critical thinking?

Bonus: Research the impact of critical thinking on
student achievement. What additional implications did
you find that were not included in the article?

Cause and Effect

A2

What are the effects of critical thinking on student learning,
according to the author? Cite evidence to support your answer.

Sequencing

A1

What is the sequence of ideas about teaching critical
thinking used in the essay? List them.

THE IMPORTANCE OF TEACHING CRITICAL THINKING

Generalizations

B3

What generalizations can you make about the importance of teaching critical thinking from the perspective of teachers? Students? Use examples from the essay and your own experiences.

Classifications

B2

How might you categorize the list of critical thinking skills mentioned in the article?

Details

B1

What are some examples of critical thinking skills from the article? Make a list for the essay.

THE IMPORTANCE OF TEACHING CRITICAL THINKING

Creative Synthesis

Participate in a quick debate with your classmates or small group on the following topic: Should we teach more critical thinking skills in schools? Provide evidence from the perspective of the author, a scientist, a businessperson hiring new graduates, and a student. Use the following chart to organize your ideas.

	Author of the Article	Scientist	Business Person	Student
Point of View				
Reasons for Their Point of View				
Implications of Their Thinking				

Summarizing

Create a new set of subtitles for the article and justify your choices.

Paraphrasing

Paraphrase the article in a paragraph.

Comparison Ladder for "Bond and Free" and "The Importance of Teaching Critical Thinking"

The importance of both the process of thinking and the thoughts that emerge cannot be understated. In each of the readings provided, students have been challenged to consider their importance. Now they have an opportunity to compare the two pieces directly.

Theme/Concept

C3

How did each author's use of language, while different, work to support his or her message? Could the same message of critical thinking be portrayed through poetry or vice versa? Explain your thinking, using evidence from each piece. Design a bumper sticker, tweet, or other short message that expresses the importance of critical thinking in our society today.

Inference

C2

The use of concepts like Love and Thought each have a role to play in the Frost poem. What function do they perform? The essay does not have characters per se. Why not? Define how a poem and an essay are different in form, based on these two examples.

Textual Elements and Understanding

C1

Summarize the main ideas of the critical thinking essay and the main ideas of the poem in a chart. How are they similar and different?

	Poem	**Essay**
Similar		
Different		

The World Is Too Much With Us
William Wordsworth

The world is too much with us; late and soon,
Getting and spending, we lay waste our powers;—
Little we see in Nature that is ours;
We have given our hearts away, a sordid boon!
This Sea that bares her bosom to the moon;
The winds that will be howling at all hours,
And are up-gathered now like sleeping flowers;
For this, for everything, we are out of tune;
It moves us not. Great God! I'd rather be
A Pagan suckled in a creed outworn;
So might I, standing on this pleasant lea,
Have glimpses that would make me less forlorn;
Have sight of Proteus rising from the sea;
Or hear old Triton blow his wreathèd horn.

Theme/Concept

C3

What does this poem suggest about progress? Write a persuasive piece in any form you wish (essay, poem, graphic organizer) to demonstrate how Wordsworth feels about progress.

Inference

C2

What does Wordsworth mean when he says "the world is too much with us"?

Textual Elements and Understanding

C1

Wordsworth was considered a Romantic poet because he emphasized the love of nature through intense emotions. What words, phrases, and rhyming patterns are used in the poem to convey his thoughts?

THE WORLD IS TOO MUCH WITH US

F3

Playing With Words

Create a prose equivalent of the poem. Analyze why you are using the punctuation you use in your prose statement.

F2

Thinking About Words

How is Wordsworth's use of punctuation to emphasize an idea similar to our use of emojis in text? What emojis would Wordsworth use if he were texting his ideas instead?

F1

Understanding Words

How does the poet evoke emotion in the poem through punctuation and other devices?

THE WORLD IS TOO MUCH WITH US

Should Schools Replace Textbooks With Tablets?

As technology progresses, more and more schools are considering the use of tablets in the classroom. Should K–12 schools shift their learning model from physical textbooks to tablet learning? There are both benefits and disadvantages to this change.

Pros

Even though tablets cost more than textbooks, they are actually the more cost-effective option over time. Each tablet has about 8–64 gigabytes of storage, meaning it can store hundreds of eBooks, as well as homework, handouts, quizzes, and other educational files. These eBooks cost about 50%–60% less than physical textbooks, so a few hundred dollars for an iPad would quickly pay off in savings. Schools would pay less for each new textbook they acquired. In addition, tablets are becoming cheaper every year, unlike textbooks. Schools could also save on paper and printing costs while helping the environment.

Benefits extend to learning as well. More and more studies are linking technology-based teaching to faster, more engaged learning. Students can work with the text in a way that ordinary books won't allow; they can highlight and edit passages, write notes, use the built-in search function and dictionary, and interact with diagrams and videos. In a recent survey, 80% of teachers reported that the use of technology enriched their classrooms while 77% reported increased motivation from the kids. Studies have also found that children with tablets read more than their nontablet peers—24 books per year rather than 15. Tablets can often make learning more fun and accessible.

The change could also benefit student health, allowing kids to carry around one lightweight tablet rather than five or more books. In 2011–2012, more than 13,700 kids were treated for backpack-related injuries. Placing materials on one device could save space and reduce back strain for children.

Tablets offer the chance for customizable learning, as each student can work at his or her own pace. There are many apps that can help teachers tailor their teaching to each individual child. With the options technology offers, education doesn't have to be one-size-fits-all.

Tablets can also allow students to keep up with changing educational and technological trends. For example, standardized testing is moving toward digital learning, and more tests will take place on computers in the coming years. By practicing and learning on tablets, students can increase their scores. Tablets could aid their long-term futures as well. By 2020, employment in computer-related fields will have risen by 18%. By allowing kids to become proficient with technology, teachers can assure that their students will be prepared for the changing, modernizing world.

Cons

Purchasing new tablets for every student would be very expensive. In addition to the tablets themselves, schools would need to pay for additional hardware and software, teacher training materials, and more elaborate Wi-Fi systems. Costs could reach $71.55 yearly for each student, compared to only $14.26 for print textbooks. Tablets would require constant recharging (most have a battery life of only 7.26 hours) and would be expensive to fix or replace if they became damaged. Theft and hacking could also become problems, since tablets are worth much more than individual books. Most schools would have difficulty meeting all of these costs.

Many parents cannot afford the upgrade either. About a third of students in the U.S. do not have broadband capabilities at home, which are needed in order operate the tablets effectively. The cost of keeping up with technology can disproportionately benefit wealthy children while neglecting poorer families. This "digital divide" grows worse when wealthier districts offer such advanced technology while poorer schools are still trying to meet basic learning needs (e.g., paper and pencils).

There are also teaching concerns about tablet technology. About 87% of teachers reported feeling that students were easily distracted and lacked focus when using technology in the classroom. The temptation to go on the Internet, check e-mail or Facebook, or play games can keep kids from learning effectively. Students could cheat more easily, looking up answers rather than working through problems step by step. The introduction of tablets can shift attention away from the teacher and toward the technology, which may impact the way that students learn and remember information.

Many studies have considered the effect that technology has on reading. People tend to read and process online material much differently than written material. According to research, online text can be more difficult to process and remember than physical text, and students also read online text more slowly. Schools should consider the health problems of Computer Vision Syndrome, which can cause headache, blurred vision, and eyestrain. The strain of leaning over screens can also lead to neck and shoulder problems.

As of 2012, only 30% of textbooks were available electronically. The numbers are expected to rise, but the remaining 70% suggests that physical books will remain important tools in teaching for quite some time.

References

Hilgedick, K. (2013). Textbooks vs. tablets: Schools begin exploring transformation in learning tools. *Jefferson City News Tribune.* Retrieved from http://www.newstribune.com/news/2013/jul/07/textbooks-vs-tablets-schools-begin-exploring-trans

ProCon.org. (2014). Should tablets replace textbooks in K–12 schools? Retrieved from http://tablets-textbooks.procon.org

Generalizations

B3

Write at least three true statements (i.e., generalizations) about the debate that could be true of either side.

Classifications

B2

Categorize what each group might believe and then make your own list of pro and con arguments based on each group's perspectives from B1.

Details

B1

Brainstorm a list of stakeholders who may be interested in this debate (e.g., students, teachers, tax payers, administration, etc.) and then outline what they might think about whether or not schools should use tablets instead of textbooks and why.

SHOULD SCHOOLS REPLACE TEXTBOOKS WITH TABLETS?

Creative Synthesis

D3

Create a slideshow presentation for your principal to convince him or her of your stance on this issue. Use no more than seven slides and make sure you explain the issue, outline the pros and cons, and provide your opinion with justification. Be convincing.

Summarizing

D2

Summarize your point of view, using evidence from the article and other information you know or research. Make sure you are citing different sources in addition to your opinion. Compare your ideas with a partner who has the opposite point of view.

Paraphrasing

D1

Create a T-chart and outline, in your own words, the pros and cons of using tablets versus textbooks from the article.

SHOULD SCHOOLS REPLACE TEXTBOOKS WITH TABLETS?

Comparison Ladder for "The World Is Too Much With Us" and "Should Schools Replace Textbooks With Tablets?"

In the 1850s, the world was experiencing the dawn of the Industrial Revolution, a precursor to our more recent technological one. Although the poem and the essay were written more than 100 years apart, there are similarities worth noting in the concerns raised. Students may now consider both the Wordsworth poem and the tablet versus text article as they complete the ladder.

Theme/Concept

C3

What do the two pieces have in common as a central message? How do they differ? Create a Venn diagram to outline the similarities and differences of the author's message in each piece. Then write a statement that would be true of both messages.

Inference

C2

What do you think Wordsworth might argue about textbooks versus tablets? Consider evidence from his poem and the time period (Industrial Revolution) in which he wrote the poem.

Textual Elements and Understanding

C1

What words and phrases are important in each piece to help you understand the main ideas?

COMPARISON LADDER FOR "THE WORLD IS TOO MUCH WITH US" AND "SHOULD SCHOOLS REPLACE TEXTBOOKS WITH TABLETS?"

Pre- and Postassessments With Scoring Rubric

Preassessment

William J. Clinton, First Inaugural Address, January 21, 1993

My fellow citizens, today we celebrate the mystery of American renewal. This ceremony is held in the depth of winter, but by the words we speak and the faces we show the world, we force the spring, a spring reborn in the world's oldest democracy that brings forth the vision and courage to reinvent America. When our Founders boldly declared America's independence to the world and our purposes to the Almighty, they knew that America, to endure, would have to change; not change for change's sake but change to preserve America's ideals: life, liberty, the pursuit of happiness. Though we marched to the music of our time, our mission is timeless. Each generation of Americans must define what it means to be an American.

On behalf of our Nation, I salute my predecessor, President Bush, for his half-century of service to America. And I thank the millions of men and women whose steadfastness and sacrifice triumphed over depression, fascism, and communism.

Today, a generation raised in the shadows of the cold war assumes new responsibilities in a world warmed by the sunshine of freedom but threatened still by ancient hatreds and new plagues. Raised in unrivaled prosperity, we inherit an economy that is still the world's strongest but is weakened by business failures, stagnant wages, increasing inequality, and deep divisions among our own people.

When George Washington first took the oath I have just sworn to uphold, news traveled slowly across the land by horseback and across the ocean by boat. Now, the sights and sounds of this ceremony are broadcast instantaneously to billions around the world. Communications and commerce are global. Investment is mobile. Technology is almost magical. And ambition for a better life is now universal.

We earn our livelihood in America today in peaceful competition with people all across the Earth. Profound and powerful forces are shaking and remaking our world. And the urgent question of our time is whether we can make change our friend and not our enemy. This new world has already enriched the lives of millions of Americans who are able to compete and win in it. But when most people are working harder for less; when others cannot work at all; when the cost of health care devastates families and threatens to bankrupt our enterprises, great and small; when the fear of crime robs law-abiding citizens of their freedom; and when millions of poor children cannot even imagine the lives we are calling them to lead, we have not made change our friend.

We know we have to face hard truths and take strong steps, but we have not done so; instead, we have drifted. And that drifting has eroded our resources, fractured our economy, and shaken our confidence. Though our challenges are fearsome, so are our strengths. Americans have ever been a restless, questing, hopeful people. And we must bring to our task today the vision and will of those who came before us. From our Revolution to the Civil War, to the Great Depression, to the Civil Rights Movement, our people have always mustered the determination to construct from these crises the pillars of our history. Thomas Jefferson believed that to preserve the very foundations of our Nation, we would need dramatic change from time to time. Well, my fellow Americans, this is our time. Let us embrace it.

Our democracy must be not only the envy of the world but the engine of our own renewal. There is nothing wrong with America that cannot be cured by what is right with America. And so today we pledge an end to the era of deadlock and drift, and a new season of American renewal has begun.

To renew America, we must be bold. We must do what no generation has had to do before. We must invest more in our own people, in their jobs, and in their future, and at the same time cut our massive debt. And we must do so in a world in which we must compete for every opportunity. It will not be easy. It will require sacrifice, but it can be done and done fairly, not choosing sacrifice for its own sake but for our own sake. We must provide for our Nation the way a family provides for its children.

Our Founders saw themselves in the light of posterity. We can do no less. Anyone who has ever watched a child's eyes wander into sleep knows what posterity is. Posterity is the world to come: the world for whom we hold our ideals, from whom we have borrowed our planet, and to whom we bear sacred responsibility. We must do what America does best: offer more opportunity to all and demand more responsibility from all. It is time to break the bad habit of expecting something for nothing from our Government or from each other. Let us all take more responsibility not only for ourselves and our families but for our communities and our country.

To renew America, we must revitalize our democracy. This beautiful Capital, like every capital since the dawn of civilization, is often a place of intrigue and calculation. Powerful people maneuver for position and worry endlessly about who is in and who is out, who is up and who is down, forgetting those people whose toil and sweat sends us here and pays our way. Americans deserve better. And in this city today there are people who want to do better. And so I say to all of you here: Let us resolve to reform our politics so that power and privilege no longer shout down the voice of the people. Let us put aside personal advantage so that we can feel the pain and see the promise of America. Let us resolve to make our Government a place for what Franklin Roosevelt called bold, persistent experimentation, a Government for our tomorrows, not our yesterdays. Let us give this Capitol back to the people to whom it belongs.

To renew America, we must meet challenges abroad as well as at home. There is no longer a clear division between what is foreign and what is domestic. The world economy, the world environment, the world AIDS crisis, the world arms race: they affect us all. Today, as an older order passes, the new world is more free but less stable. Communism's collapse has called forth old animosities and new dangers. Clearly, America must continue to lead the world we did so much to make.

While America rebuilds at home, we will not shrink from the challenges nor fail to seize the opportunities of this new world. Together with our friends and allies, we will work to shape change, lest it engulf us. When our vital interests are challenged or the will and conscience of the international community is defied, we will act, with peaceful diplomacy whenever possible, with force when necessary. The brave Americans serving our Nation today in the Persian Gulf, in Somalia, and wherever else they stand are testament to our resolve. But our greatest strength is the power of our ideas, which are still new in many lands. Across the world we see them embraced, and we rejoice. Our hopes, our hearts, our hands are with those on every continent who are building democracy and freedom. Their cause is America's cause.

The American people have summoned the change we celebrate today. You have raised your voices in an unmistakable chorus. You have cast your votes in historic numbers. And you have changed the face of Congress, the Presidency, and the political process itself. Yes, you, my fellow Americans, have forced the spring. Now we must do the work the season demands. To that work I now turn with all the authority of my office. I ask the Congress to join with me. But no President, no Congress, no Government can undertake this mission alone.

My fellow Americans, you, too, must play your part in our renewal. I challenge a new generation of young Americans to a season of service: to act on your idealism by helping troubled children, keeping company with those in need, reconnecting our torn communities. There is so much to be done; enough, indeed, for millions of others who are still young in spirit to give of themselves in service, too. In serving, we recognize a simple but powerful truth: We need each other, and we must care for one another.

Today we do more than celebrate America. We rededicate ourselves to the very idea of America, an idea born in revolution and renewed through two centuries of challenge; an idea tempered by the knowledge that, but for fate, we, the fortunate, and the unfortunate might have been each other; an idea ennobled by the faith that our Nation can summon from its myriad diversity the deepest measure of unity; an idea infused with the conviction that America's long, heroic journey must go forever upward.

And so, my fellow Americans, as we stand at the edge of the 21st century, let us begin anew with energy and hope, with faith and discipline. And let us work until our work is done. The Scripture says, "And let us not be weary in well doing: for in due season we shall reap, if we faint not." From this joyful mountaintop of celebration we hear a call to service in the valley. We have heard the trumpets. We have changed the guard. And now, each in our own way and with God's help, we must answer the call.

Thank you, and God bless you all.

Note. From "First Inaugural Address," by W. J. Clinton, 1993, retrieved from http://www.presidency.ucsb.edu/ws/?pid=46366. Reprinted from the public domain.

Preassessment: Questions

Read and answer each question using evidence from the speech to support your ideas.

1. What are the positive and negative consequences of living in America at this current time, according to Bill Clinton?

    _____

    _____

    _____

    _____

    _____

    _____

2. Write at least two true generalizations about Clinton's assessment of America. Explain why these statements are true, using evidence from the speech.

    _____

    _____

    _____

    _____

    _____

    _____

Name: _____ Date: _____

3. What does Clinton mean when he says "Our democracy must be not only the envy of the world but the engine of our own renewal. There is nothing wrong with America that cannot be cured by what is right with America"? Paraphrase his statement in your own words.

_____

_____

_____

_____

_____

_____

4. Create a new title for this speech and justify why this title is a good one, based on what you have read.

_____

_____

_____

_____

_____

_____

Postassessment

George W. Bush First Inaugural Address, January 20, 2001

Thank you, all. Chief Justice Rehnquist, President Carter, President Bush, President Clinton, distinguished guests, and my fellow citizens. The peaceful transfer of authority is rare in history, yet common in our country. With a simple oath, we affirm old traditions and make new beginnings.

As I begin, I thank President Clinton for his service to our Nation, and I thank Vice President Gore for a contest conducted with spirit and ended with grace.

I am honored and humbled to stand here where so many of America's leaders have come before me, and so many will follow. We have a place, all of us, in a long story, a story we continue but whose end we will not see. It is a story of a new world that became a friend and liberator of the old, the story of a slaveholding society that became a servant of freedom, the story of a power that went into the world to protect but not possess, to defend but not to conquer.

It is the American story, a story of flawed and fallible people united across the generations by grand and enduring ideals. The grandest of these ideals is an unfolding American promise that everyone belongs, that everyone deserves a chance, that no insignificant person was ever born.

Americans are called to enact this promise in our lives and in our laws. And though our Nation has sometimes halted and sometimes delayed, we must follow no other course.

Through much of the last century, America's faith in freedom and democracy was a rock in a raging sea. Now it is a seed upon the wind, taking root in many nations. Our democratic faith is more than the creed of our country. It is the inborn hope of our humanity, an ideal we carry but do not own, a trust we bear and pass along. Even after nearly 225 years, we have a long way yet to travel.

While many of our citizens prosper, others doubt the promise, even the justice of our own country. The ambitions of some Americans are limited by failing schools and hidden prejudice and the circumstances of their birth. And sometimes our differences run so deep, it seems we share a continent but not a country. We do not accept this, and we will not allow it.

Our unity, our Union, is a serious work of leaders and citizens and every generation. And this is my solemn pledge: I will work to build a single nation of justice and opportunity. I know this is in our reach because we are guided by a power larger than ourselves, who creates us equal, in His image, and we are confident in principles that unite and lead us onward.

America has never been united by blood or birth or soil. We are bound by ideals that move us beyond our backgrounds, lift us above our interests, and teach us what it means to be citizens. Every child must be taught these principles. Every citizen must uphold them. And every immigrant, by embracing these ideals, makes our country more, not less, American.

Today we affirm a new commitment to live out our Nation's promise through civility, courage, compassion, and character. America at its best matches a commitment to principle with a concern for civility. A civil society demands from each of us good will and respect, fair dealing and forgiveness.

Some seem to believe that our politics can afford to be petty because in a time of peace the stakes of our debates appear small. But the stakes for America are never small. If our country does not lead the cause of freedom, it will not be led. If we do not turn the hearts of children toward knowledge and character, we will lose their gifts and undermine their idealism. If we permit our economy to drift and decline, the vulnerable will suffer most.

We must live up to the calling we share. Civility is not a tactic or a sentiment; it is the determined choice of trust over cynicism, of community over chaos. And this commitment, if we keep it, is a way to shared accomplishment.

America at its best is also courageous. Our national courage has been clear in times of depression and war, when defeating common dangers defined our common good. Now we must choose if the example of our fathers and mothers will inspire us or condemn us. We must show courage in a time of blessing by confronting problems instead of passing them on to future generations.

Together we will reclaim America's schools before ignorance and apathy claim more young lives. We will reform Social Security and Medicare, sparing our children from struggles we have the power to prevent. And we will reduce taxes to recover the momentum of our economy and reward the effort and enterprise of working Americans.

We will build our defenses beyond challenge, lest weakness invite challenge. We will confront weapons of mass destruction, so that a new century is spared new horrors. The enemies of liberty and our country should make no mistake: America remains engaged in the world, by history and by choice, shaping a balance of power that favors freedom.

We will defend our allies and our interests. We will show purpose without arrogance. We will meet aggression and bad faith with resolve and strength. And to all nations, we will speak for the values that gave our Nation birth.

America at its best is compassionate. In the quiet of American conscience, we know that deep, persistent poverty is unworthy of our Nation's promise. And whatever our views of its cause, we can agree that children at risk are not at fault.

Abandonment and abuse are not acts of God; they are failures of love. And the proliferation of prisons, however necessary, is no substitute for hope and order in our souls. Where there is suffering, there is duty. Americans in need are not strangers; they are citizens—not problems but priorities. And all of us are diminished when any are hopeless.

Government has great responsibilities for public safety and public health, for civil rights and common schools. Yet, compassion is the work of a nation, not just a government. And some needs and hurts are so deep they will only respond to a mentor's touch or a pastor's prayer. Church and charity, synagogue and mosque lend our communities their humanity, and they will have an honored place in our plans and in our laws.

Many in our country do not know the pain of poverty. But we can listen to those who do. And I can pledge our Nation to a goal: When we see that wounded traveler on the road to Jericho, we will not pass to the other side.

America at its best is a place where personal responsibility is valued and expected. Encouraging responsibility is not a search for scapegoats; it is a call to conscience. And though it requires sacrifice, it brings a deeper fulfillment. We find the fullness of life not only in options but in commitments. And we find that children and community are the commitments that set us free.

Our public interest depends on private character, on civic duty and family bonds and basic fairness, on uncounted, unhonored acts of decency, which give direction to our freedom.

Sometimes in life we're called to do great things. But as a saint of our times has said, "Every day we are called to do small things with great love." The most important tasks of a democracy are done by everyone.

I will live and lead by these principles: to advance my convictions with civility, to serve the public interest with courage, to speak for greater justice and compassion, to call for responsibility and try to live it, as well. In all these ways, I will bring the values of our history to the care of our times.

What you do is as important as anything Government does. I ask you to seek a common good beyond your comfort, to defend needed reforms against easy attacks, to serve your Nation, beginning with your neighbor. I ask you to be citizens: Citizens, not spectators; citizens, not subjects; responsible citizens building communities of service and a nation of character.

Americans are generous and strong and decent, not because we believe in ourselves but because we hold beliefs beyond ourselves. When this spirit of citizenship is missing, no Government program can replace it. When this spirit is present, no wrong can stand against it.

After the Declaration of Independence was signed, Virginia statesman John Page wrote to Thomas Jefferson, "We know the race is not to the swift, nor the battle to the strong. Do you not think an angel rides in the whirlwind and directs this storm?"

Much time has passed since Jefferson arrived for his inauguration. The years and changes accumulate, but the themes of this day, he would know: our Nation's grand story of courage and its simple dream of dignity.

We are not this story's author, who fills time and eternity with his purpose. Yet, his purpose is achieved in our duty. And our duty is fulfilled in service to one another. Never tiring, never yielding, never finishing, we renew that purpose today, to make our country more just and generous, to affirm the dignity of our lives and every life. This work continues, the story goes on, and an angel still rides in the whirlwind and directs this storm.

God bless you all, and God bless America.

Note. From "First Inaugural Address," by G. W. Bush, 2001, retrieved from http://www.presidency.ucsb.edu/ws/?pid=25853. Reprinted from the public domain.

Postassessment: Questions

Read and answer each question using evidence from the speech to support your ideas.

1. What are the positive and negative consequences of living in America at this current time, according to George W. Bush?

    _____

    _____

    _____

    _____

    _____

    _____

2. Write at least two generalizations about Bush's assessment of the needs of America. Explain why these statements are true, using evidence from the speech.

    _____

    _____

    _____

    _____

    _____

    _____

Name: _____ Date: _____

3. What does Bush mean when he says "America has never been united by blood or birth or soil. We are bound by ideals that move us beyond our backgrounds, lift us above our interests and teach us what it means to be citizens. Every child must be taught these principles. Every citizen must uphold them. And every immigrant, by embracing these ideals, makes our country more, not less, American"? Paraphrase the comment in your own words.

_____

_____

_____

_____

_____

_____

4. Create a new title for this speech and justify why this title is a good one, based on what you have read.

_____

_____

_____

_____

_____

_____

Assessment Scoring Rubric

Question	Points				
	0	1	2	3	4
1 **Implications and Consequences (Ladder A)**	Provides no response or response is inappropriate to the task demand	Limited, vague, inaccurate; rewords the prompt or copies from the text	Response is somewhat accurate and makes sense but does not adequately address all components of the question or provide rationale from the text	Response is accurate; answers all parts of the question; provides a rationale that justifies the response but lacks interpretation or thorough evidence	Response is well written, specific, logical, interpretive; correctly answers all parts of the question, incorporates thorough evidence from the text
2 **Generalization (Ladder B)**	Provides no response or response is inappropriate to the task demand	Limited, vague, inaccurate; rewords the prompt or copies from text	Response is accurate but the generalizations are literal and limited	Generalizations are accurate and mostly synthesize the text but lack thorough justification or complete synthesis	Generalizations are interpretive with substantial justification or reasoning from the text
3 **Inference (Ladder C)**	Provides no response or response is inappropriate to the task demand	Limited, vague, inaccurate; rewords the prompt or copies from text	Accurate response but literal interpretation with no support from the text	Somewhat interpretive response but incomplete or with limited support from the text	Interpretive response with substantial support from the text
4 **Creative Synthesis (Ladder D)**	Provides no response or response is inappropriate to the task demand	Limited, vague, inaccurate; rewords the prompt or copies a phrase from text	Appropriate but literal title with little to no support	Interpretive title with limited reasoning or justification	Interpretive title that synthesizes the meaning of the piece, and uses extensive justification or reasoning from text

APPENDIX
B

Record-Keeping Forms/Documents

This section includes a record-keeping sheet for each section. The forms can be used to keep track of student understanding and higher level thinking as they discuss different ladders or rungs. These may also be used in conjunction with the preassessments to diagnose and prescribe specific ladders based on student responses to each question by matching their response on each pretest question to a corresponding ladder and reading selection as part of differentiation.

Appendix B contains three record-keeping forms and documents:

- *Brainstorming/Answer Sheet*: This should be given to students for completion after reading a selection so that they may jot down ideas about the selection and questions prior to the discussion. The purpose of this sheet is to capture students' thoughts and ideas generated by reading the text. This sheet should act as a guide when students participate in group or class discussion.

- *My Reflection on Today's Reading and Discussion*: This form may be completed by the student after a group or class discussion on the readings. The reflection page is designed as a metacognitive approach to help students reflect on their strengths and weaknesses and to promote process skills. After discussion, students use the reflection page to record new ideas that were generated by others' comments and ideas.

- *Classroom Diagnostic Form*: These forms are for teachers and are designed to aid them in keeping track of the progress and skill mastery of their students. With these charts, teachers can look at student progress in relation to each ladder skill within a genre and select additional ladders and story selections based on student needs.

Brainstorming/Answer Sheet

Use this form to brainstorm thoughts and ideas about the readings and ladder questions before discussing with a partner.

Selection Title: _____

Circle One: **A3 B3 C3 D3 E3 F3**

Circle One: **A2 B2 C2 D2 E2 F2**

Circle One: **A1 B1 C1 D1 E1 F1**

My Reflection on Today's Reading and Discussion

Selection Title: _____

What I did well:

_____

_____

_____

_____

What I learned:

_____

_____

_____

_____

New ideas I have after discussion:

_____

_____

_____

_____

Next time I need to:

_____

_____

_____

_____

Classroom Diagnostic Form

Section 1: Science

Use this document to record student completion of ladder sets with the assessment of work.

0 = Needs Improvement   1 = Satisfactory   2 = Exceeds Expectations

Student Name	Summary of the Clean Air Act			Flint's Water Crisis			Four New Elements Added to the Periodic Table			Astronomers Discover Signs of Milky Way's Second Largest Black Hole			Mindsets: How the Popular Psychological Theory Relates to Success			Excerpt From "The Fringe Benefits of Failure and the Importance of Imagination"		
	A	D	B (Comp. Ladder)	A	C	B (Comp. Ladder)	C	D	C	B	C	B	B	C (Comp. Ladder)	B	E	C (Comp. Ladder)

Classroom Diagnostic Form

Section 2: Math

Use this document to record student completion of ladder sets with the assessment of work.

0 = Needs Improvement   1 = Satisfactory   2 = Exceeds Expectations

Student Name	How Old Are You—in Seconds?		What's the Biggest Number?		George Boole and the Wonderful World of 0s and 1s		Focus on the Global Economy	
	A	B (Comp. Ladder)	C	B (Comp. Ladder)	A	B	A	D

Classroom Diagnostic Form

Section 3: Social Studies

Use this document to record student completion of ladder sets with the assessment of work.

0 = Needs Improvement   1 = Satisfactory   2 = Exceeds Expectations

Student Name	Excerpt From "Seeing Red: The Cold War and American Public Opinion"		Excerpt From "Their Finest Hour"			Woman's Rights to the Suffrage				Ain't I a Woman?		
	B	D	A	B	D	A	D	D (Comp. Ladder)		B	E	D (Comp. Ladder)

Classroom Diagnostic Form

Section 4: The Arts

Use this document to record student completion of ladder sets with the assessment of work.

0 = Needs Improvement   1 = Satisfactory   2 = Exceeds Expectations

Student Name	Excerpt From William Faulkner Nobel Prize Banquet Speech, 1950				Excerpt From Mario Vargas Llosa Nobel Prize Banquet Speech, 2010				Remains of the Past: Roman Art and Architecture			Jacob Lawrence		Duke Ellington	
	A	C	C (Comp. Ladder)	D (Comp. Ladder)	A	C	C (Comp. Ladder)	D (Comp. Ladder)	A	B	A	B	C	A	D

Classroom Diagnostic Form

Part III: Fiction and Nonfiction Comparisons

Use this document to record student completion of ladder sets with the assessment of work.

0 = Needs Improvement   1 = Satisfactory   2 = Exceeds Expectations

| Student Name | Break, Break, Break | | | Korean War Photo Analysis | | | Composed Upon Westminster Bridge, September 3, 1802 | | | William Wordsworth | | At the Window | | D. H. Lawrence | |
	D	F	E (Comp. Ladder)	C	E (Comp. Ladder)	C	F	C (Comp. Ladder)	A	C (Comp. Ladder)	A	B (Comp. Ladder)	C	B (Comp. Ladder)

Classroom Diagnostic Form, Part III: Fiction and Nonfiction Comparisons, *continued*

Student Name	Bond and Free			The Importance of Critical Thinking				The World Is Too Much With Us			Should Schools Replace Textbooks With Tablets?		
	C	D	C (Comp. Ladder)	A	B	D	C (Comp. Ladder)	C	F	C (Comp. Ladder)	B	D	C (Comp. Ladder)

APPENDIX
C

Common Core State Standards Alignment

The alignment of the Jacob's Ladder nonfiction books to the Common Core State Standards (CCSS) may be best understood by examining the relevant sections of the ELA Nonfiction standards by grade level first, and seeing the corresponding ladders that require students to discuss and answer questions and do activities that address the standard under consideration.

Secondly, it is also important to review the textual choices selected, as many are advanced in reading level for the cited grade-level designation. For example, the following standards are cited as grade 5, yet many of the selected readings used are pitched two or more grade levels above, demonstrating the accelerated reading component of the program. Because many of the readings are accelerated, the processes, concepts, and activities required are also accelerated and may meet partial or full standards in ELA above grade 5, too.

Thirdly, it is useful to consider each of the subject matter standards as well for coverage, as we have deliberately organized these books by subject area categories to diversify the readings and relate to the standards in each domain. For example, the use of the speeches of U.S. presidents meets the ELA standards for drawing inferences from text, determining main ideas, and explaining relationships between concepts, among others, in history. It also meets the social studies standards for analyzing events and individuals in history. The same may be true for science and math, especially as the standards call for the use of reasoning, scientific process skill sets, and interpreting authors' opinions/findings versus facts.

Finally, it is important to note that not all reading selections will have questions and activities that correspond to the ladders noted in the chart. We have indicated a correspondence if several selections have ladders that consistently make the connection to the standard cited. Other outcomes may be fulfilled for certain ladders, although not specifically listed. Moreover, merely having one match does not mean that a standard has been fully addressed. Teacher judgment needs to prevail in how much practice is needed in the type of higher order skills that these standards and ladders constitute, as well as which outcomes are best suited for a particular reading and ladder.

Common Core State Standards Alignment	A	B	C	D	E	F
Reading: Key Ideas & Details						
CCSS.ELA-Literacy.RI.5.1 Quote accurately from a text when explaining what the text says explicitly and when drawing inferences from the text.			X	X		
CCSS.ELA-Literacy.RI.5.2 Determine two or more main ideas of a text and explain how they are supported by key details; summarize the text.		X		X		
CCSS.ELA-Literacy.RI.5.3 Explain the relationships or interactions between two or more individuals, events, ideas, or concepts in a historical, scientific, or technical text based on specific information in the text.	X	X	X			
Reading: Craft & Structure						
CCSS.ELA-Literacy.RI.5.4 Determine the meaning of general academic and domain-specific words and phrases in a text relevant to a grade 5 topic or subject area.				X		
CCSS.ELA-Literacy.RI.5.5 Compare and contrast the overall structure (e.g., chronology, comparison, cause/effect, problem/solution) of events, ideas, concepts, or information in two or more texts.	X	X	X	X		
CCSS.ELA-Literacy.RI.5.6 Analyze multiple accounts of the same event or topic, noting important similarities and differences in the point of view they represent.	X	X	X			
Reading: Integration of Knowledge & Ideas						
CCSS.ELA-Literacy.RI.5.7 Draw on information from multiple print or digital sources, demonstrating the ability to locate an answer to a question quickly or to solve a problem efficiently.	X			X		

Commmon Core State Standards Alignment

Commmon Core State Standards Alignment	A	B	C	D	E	F
CCSS.ELA-Literacy.RI.5.8 Explain how an author uses reasons and evidence to support particular points in a text, identifying which reasons and evidence support which point(s).	✗	✗	✗			
CCSS.ELA-Literacy.RI.5.9 Integrate information from several texts on the same topic in order to write or speak about the subject knowledgeably.	✗	✗	✗			
Reading: Range of Reading & Level of Text Complexity						
CCSS.ELA-Literacy.RI.5.10 By the end of the year, read and comprehend informational texts, including history/social studies, science, and technical texts, at the high end of the grades 4–5 text complexity band independently and proficiently.	✗	✗	✗	✗	✗	✗
Writing						
CCSS.ELA-Literacy.W.5.1 Write opinion pieces on topics or texts, supporting a point of view with reasons and information.	✗		✗	✗	✗	
CCSS.ELA-Literacy.W.5.2 Write informative/explanatory texts to examine a topic and convey ideas and information clearly.			✗	✗		
CCSS.ELA-Literacy.W.5.3 Write narratives to develop real or imagined experiences or events using effective technique, descriptive details, and clear event sequences.				✗		
Research: Research to Build and Present Knowledge						
CCSS.ELA-Literacy.W.5.7 Conduct short research projects that use several sources to build knowledge through investigation of different aspects of a topic.				✗		

Common Core State Standards Alignment	A	B	C	D	E	F
CCSS.ELA-Literacy.W.5.8 Recall relevant information from experiences or gather relevant information from print and digital sources; summarize or paraphrase information in notes and finished work, and provide a list of sources.				X		
CCSS.ELA-Literacy.W.5.9 Draw evidence from literary or informational texts to support analysis, reflection, and research.	X	X	X	X		
Speaking & Listening: Comprehension and Collaboration						
CCSS.ELA-Literacy.SL.5.1 Engage effectively in a range of collaborative discussions (one-on-one, in groups, and teacher-led) with diverse partners on grade 5 topics and texts, building on others' ideas and expressing their own clearly.	X	X	X	X	X	X
CCSS.ELA-Literacy.SL.5.3 Summarize the points a speaker makes and explain how each claim is supported by reasons and evidence.				X		
Speaking & Listening: Presentation of Knowledge and Ideas						
CCSS.ELA-Literacy.SL.5.4 Report on a topic or text or present an opinion, sequencing ideas logically and using appropriate facts and relevant, descriptive details to support main ideas or themes; speak clearly at an understandable pace.			X			
CCSS.ELA-Literacy.SL.5.5 Include multimedia components (e.g., graphics, sound) and visual displays in presentations when appropriate to enhance the development of main ideas or themes.			X	X		
CCSS.ELA-Literacy.SL.5.6 Adapt speech to a variety of contexts and tasks, using formal English when appropriate to task and situation. (See grade 5 Language standards 1 and 3 here for specific expectations.)	X	X	X	X	X	X

About the Authors

Joyce VanTassel-Baska, Ed.D., is the Jody and Layton Smith Professor Emerita of Education and founding director of the Center for Gifted Education at The College of William and Mary in Virginia where she developed a graduate program and a research and development center in gifted education. She also initiated and directed the Center for Talent Development at Northwestern University. Prior to her work in higher education, Dr. VanTassel-Baska served as the state director of gifted programs for Illinois, as a regional director of a gifted service center in the Chicago area, as coordinator of gifted programs for the Toledo, Ohio public school system, and as a teacher of gifted high school students in English and Latin. She has worked as a consultant on gifted education in all 50 states and for key national groups, including the U.S. Department of Education, National Association of Secondary School Principals, and American Association of School Administrators. She has consulted internationally in Australia, New Zealand, Hungary, Jordan, Singapore, Korea, Hong Kong, China, England, Germany, The Netherlands, Spain, Kazakhstan, Oman, and the United Arab Emirates. She is past president of The Association for the Gifted, the Council for Exceptional Children, the Northwestern University Chapter of Phi Delta Kappa, and the National Association for Gifted Children (NAGC). During her tenure as NAGC president, she oversaw the adoption of the new teacher standards for gifted education, and organized and chaired the National Leadership Conference on Promising and Low-Income Learners.

Dr. VanTassel-Baska has published widely, including 30 books and more than 550 refereed journal articles, book chapters, and scholarly reports. Recent books include: *Content-Based Curriculum for Gifted Learners* (3rd edition; 2016; with Catherine Little), *Patterns and Profiles of Low Income Learners* (2010), *Social and Emotional Curriculum for Gifted and Talented Students* (2009; with Tracy Cross and Rick Olenchak), *Alternative Assessment With Gifted Students* (2008), *Serving Gifted Learners Beyond the Traditional Classroom* (2007), and *Comprehensive Curriculum for Gifted Education* (3rd edition; 2006; with Tamra Stambaugh). Recent curriculum work includes The Jacob's Ladder Reading Comprehension Program (with Tamra Stambaugh), units of study on leadership (with Linda Avery) and on Rome, focusing on its language, history, and art and architecture (with Ariel Baska). She also served as the editor of *Gifted and Talented International*, a research journal of the World Council on Gifted and Talented, for 7 years from 1998–2005.

Dr. VanTassel-Baska has received numerous awards for her work, including the National Association for Gifted Children's Early Leader Award in 1986; the State Council of Higher Education in Virginia Outstanding Faculty Award in 1993; the Phi Beta Kappa faculty award in 1995; the National Association for Gifted Children Distinguished Scholar Award in 1997; the President's Award, World Council on Gifted and Talented Education in 2005; the Distinguished Service Award, CEC-TAG, in 2007; and was inducted as an American Educational Research Association (AERA) Fellow in 2010 along with receiving the Distinguished Service Award from NAGC in the same year. In 2011, she received the Mensa Award for Lifetime Achievement in research and service to gifted education. In 2013, she received the Distinguished Service Award from The World Council on the Gifted and Talented. In 2014, she received the Legacy Award from NAGC for her lifetime contribution to gifted education and a recognition award from Rutgers University for her work in establishing gifted education coursework at that institution. She also has received awards from five states— Ohio, Virginia, Colorado, South Carolina, and Illinois—for her contribution to the field of gifted education in those states. She was selected as a Fulbright Scholar to New Zealand in 2000 and a visiting scholar to Cambridge University in England in 1993. Her major research interests are on the talent development process and effective curricular interventions with the gifted. She has served as principal investigator on 65 grants and contracts totaling more than $15 million, including eight from the United States Department of Education (USDOE). She holds B.A., M.A., M.Ed., and Ed.D. degrees from the University of Toledo, an institution that awarded her its Distinguished Achievement Alumna Award in 2002.

Tamra Stambaugh, Ph.D., is an assistant research professor in special education and executive director of Programs for Talented Youth at Vanderbilt University. Stambaugh conducts research in gifted education with a focus on students living in rural settings, students of poverty, and curriculum and instructional interventions that promote gifted student learning. She is the coauthor/editor of several books, including *Comprehensive Curriculum for Gifted Learners* (2007; with Joyce VanTassel-Baska); *Overlooked Gems: A National Perspective on Low-Income Promising Students* (2007; with Joyce VanTassel-Baska), *Leading Change in Gifted Education* (2009; with Bronwyn MacFarlane), the Jacob's Ladder Reading Comprehension Program Series (2008, 2009, 2010, 2011, 2012, 2016; with Joyce VanTassel-Baska), *Effective Curriculum for Underserved Gifted Students* (2012; with Kim Chandler), *Serving Gifted Students in Rural Settings* (Legacy Award Winner; with Susannah Wood), and the ELA Lessons for Gifted and Advanced Learners in Grades 6–8 series (2016; with Emily Mofield). Stambaugh has also written numerous articles and book chapters. She frequently provides keynotes, professional development workshops, and consultation to school districts nationally and internationally and shares her work at refereed research conferences. She serves on the National Association for Gifted Children (NAGC) awards and professional standards committees and is a reviewer for leading research journals in the field of gifted education.

Stambaugh is the recipient of several awards including: the Margaret The Lady Thatcher Medallion for scholarship, service, and character from the College of William and Mary School of Education; the Doctoral Student Award, Early Leader Award, and several curriculum awards from the National Association for Gifted Children; the Jo Patterson Service Award and Curriculum Award from the Tennessee Association for Gifted Children; and the Higher Education Award from the Ohio Association for Gifted Children. Stambaugh has received or directed research and service grants totaling more than $7.5 million. Prior to her appointment at Vanderbilt, she was director of grants and special projects at the College of William and Mary, Center for Gifted Education where she earned her Ph.D.